GRACE
where you are

GRACE
where you are

EMILY BELLE FREEMAN

DESERET
BOOK

For Meg and Sam and all those who are
burdened by the weight of after all you can do.
Come, discover His grace.

Interior Illustrations: Allison Kimball
Other Artwork: Aleksandr Simono/Shutterstock.com; ESB Professional/Shutterstock.com
Endsheets: Slanapotam/Getty Images

Visit us at deseretbook.com

Library of Congress Cataloging-in-Publication Data

Names: Freeman, Emily, 1969– author.
Title: Grace where you are / Emily Belle Freeman.
Description: Salt Lake City, Utah : Deseret Book, [2020] | Includes bibliographical references. | Summary: "Bestselling Latter-day Saint author Emily Belle Freeman explains the concept of grace and how it works in our everyday lives"—Provided by publisher.
Identifiers: LCCN 2019054791 | ISBN 9781629727271 (hardcover)
Subjects: LCSH: The Church of Jesus Christ of Latter-day Saints—Doctrines. | Atonement—The Church of Jesus Christ of Latter-day Saints. | Grace (Theology) | Christian life—Mormon authors. | Mormon Church—Doctrines.
Classification: LCC BX8643.A85 F74 2020 | DDC 234/.1—dc23
LC record available at https://lccn.loc.gov/2019054791

Printed in the United States of America
Lake Book Manufacturing, Inc., Melrose Park, IL

10 9 8 7 6 5 4 3 2

CONTENTS

CONTENTS

Where It Begins

She stands right next to the conductor under the bright lights of the stage. Hair done up, wearing her best green dress, one hand grasping her violin, the other moving lightning fast with the bow. A child prodigy of fourteen, playing with the Boston Symphony as if she were a master, and yet she will still have to ride home from the symphony hall with her mom.

The audience watches transfixed as the little girl in the green dress performs from the center of the stage. Somewhere near the end it happens, in the crescendo of Leonard Bernstein's *Serenade*. The E string of her violin snaps, and Midori is left standing center stage with a broken instrument.

The symphony continues; the conductor is still waving his arms, the performers following his lead.

In that split second, Midori walks over to the concertmaster, who hands her his very own violin, and she begins to play again—her bow, her heart, every breath in rhythm with the conductor. The concertmaster's Stradivarius violin makes it only a few more stanzas before the E string snaps again. One more time, Midori walks over to the concertmaster. He hands her another violin so she will be able to finish out the performance. Again, she doesn't miss a beat. If you hadn't been watching closely you might not have even noticed. But Midori remembers it clearly. Years later she thought back to that moment. "Everything happened very fast," she recalls with a gentle smile. "It's not the most comfortable thing to play on somebody else's instrument, especially when I was so attached to my own instrument. To have to switch instruments is not an easy thing."[1]

I watch the performance and I can't help but consider Midori's heart. I don't play the violin. But life has taught me what it is to hold a broken instrument, to hear the symphony continuing on without me, to consider giving up and walking off the stage. I know what uncomfortable feels like. It is within these moments that I, too, have come to know my Concertmaster. The One who is always watching, waiting, ready with another instrument in hand. Like Paul, I am confident of "this very thing, that he which hath begun a good work in [me] will perform it" (Philippians 1:6).

Even when I feel broken.

Especially when I feel broken.

He waits, right there where I am, in the center of my own story, ready for those broken moments. He knows there will be broken moments. *He knows there will be more than one.* But this Concertmaster doesn't hold out a violin; instead He offers grace.

Grace where you are.

---

1. https://www.youtube.com/watch?v=jDQp8iJRqTY.

And maybe it feels unfamiliar. Maybe grace doesn't feel comfortable. Maybe learning grace is a symphony you haven't yet mastered.

Perhaps you wonder what grace is.

If so, then this is the perfect place to begin.

I am not an expert on grace, but my life has been filled to overflowing with broken—the kind of broken that has led me to the Concertmaster time after time after time.

Those experiences have burned within and whispered to my soul to write. I want to share my journey with you, a journey filled with evidence of the Grace Giver. How He speaks through the sunrise, how He signals through the storm, how He watches over through the deepest dark of night.

How He comes.

Like Paul, I want to "finish my course with joy, and the ministry, which I have received of the Lord Jesus, to testify . . . of grace" (Acts 20:24). I pray that somewhere within these pages I will find the words to witness of His grace in my life.

There are some things in life I am certain of. Grace is one of those things. Here is what I believe: Grace is not just for the salvation of sinners, but also for the bestowal of blessings. It is given through the Atonement of Jesus Christ. He was willing to come down, and come in, to help each of us become. His grace is the gift of transformation. An endowment of strength. Divine assistance. An enabling power. The elevating of souls and the healing of hearts. Grace is His favor, and His kindness, and the tenderness with which He extends His mercies. It is His touch on our heart and how we reflect that within our life. Grace is always there, but we notice it most in our weakness. In our brokenness.

Receiving grace isn't an event. It's a story.

It's my story, and it's your story.

And it can happen now. In this split second. Because the Concertmaster is willing to give up His own instrument for you. He is offering His best. He wants to repair whatever is broken in you with His grace.

Right here.

Where you are.

"GRACE BE WITH YOU."

—2 TIMOTHY 4:22

This place where you
are in your story?
This is where
grace begins...

Part One

understanding grace

chapter one

A Gift of Radical Generosity

Our family is growing. There are new spouses and new babies, and I often find myself window-shopping for kitchen tables. I long for a gathering place with good food and good conversation—the place we circle 'round. It has become an obsession, creating this space. Thoughts of it fill my daydreaming. Enough chairs for everyone, dinner plates laid out on the table. Matching silverware, crystal glasses filled with ice water, warm rolls and soft butter. Light from the windows filtering through the white blinds, and we are all here together.

Perhaps I am not the only one with this dream.

Once a certain man decided to host a great supper. The table was set—food overflowing in abundance, glasses topped off, candles lit. The invitations had been delivered weeks before. The day of the event was filled with preparations for the celebration. Once everything was ready, a servant was sent to tell all the people to come, but each guest had an excuse—I have bought a piece of ground, I have bought five yoke of oxen, I have married a wife. It was the business of everyday life. *And what keeps you from feasting with the Lord?*

The servant returned home alone. He looked at the great feast laid out on the table, at each of the empty chairs, at the lord standing in anticipation at the head of the table, and then he shared the news: no one would be coming. It must have been discouraging, but the master of the house responded instantly, "Go . . . and *bring* . . . the poor, and the maimed, and the halt, and the blind" (Luke 14:21; emphasis added). And so, the servant went. I can't help but wonder, did he dress the poor one, and carry the crippled one? Did he lend a hand to the limping one and lead the blind one carefully to his chair? Once they were all settled, the servant turned to the lord again, saying, "I have done as you asked *and still there is room*." The lord replied, "Go out into the highways and hedges and *compel them to come in*, that my house may be filled" (vv. 22–23; emphasis added). *Go*, he said, *find the people in the margins. They won't want to come; perhaps they will think they aren't worthy of such a feast. Beg them to come. Compel them. Tell them I want them here. Fill up my house with them* (see Luke 14:17–23).

I can't help but notice how the lord empowers the servant with the spirit of radical generosity—so different from the usual generosity, offered to all and marked by abundance. Welcoming. Inviting. Can't you just imagine the servant extending the invitation to every soul in the town—the broken, the sick, and those in the margins? Some called them misfits; Christ called them chosen. I try to imagine what the people looked like who sat around the table that night. I picture what they might have been wearing. I imagine their clothes were torn, their faces were dirty, perhaps even their hair was unkempt. But one thing is certain—they were filled.

One time when I was reading this story, a good friend leaned over and asked me a question I have never forgotten: "What do you think the man was serving? At the supper. What was he serving at the feast?"

"I don't know," I replied, "I don't think it tells us."

"Oh, it does," he answered, "Look carefully. What were they hungry for? The poor, the maimed, the halt, the blind, the marginalized."

I looked again, and he whispered the answer. "Healing."

The gift the Grace Giver bestows abundantly.

It is a beautiful lesson. All are invited to His feast. Everyone is welcome. But there is a greater lesson here that is still true today—when Jesus comes to the table, He looks around to see who is missing, and then He starts extending invitations. He is the Savior, the Giver of Grace, and He wants everyone to partake of the gift He offers—deliverance, protection, healing, preservation, even being made whole. *Everyone.*

The house is quiet. I sit in my favorite chair and listen to a song entitled "Come to the Table," by the Sidewalk Prophets. It is a song of invitation, a welcome. Somehow this songwriter has found a way to list every single person you can imagine, and as he mentions each of them, my mind fills with pictures—thieves, doubters, heroes, cowards, prisoners, soldiers, paupers, princes, the loved, the lost, followers, and leaders. He remembers those who hunger and thirst, those who feel left out, and those who love. He mentions the wanderers, the dreamers, and the sufferers. The young and the old. *He remembers everyone.* In my mind's eye, I picture each of those people, I see them there in their places, and I realize an important truth: the invitation to receive grace is extended to each of us in whatever place we are in. "Come to the table, dear friend. Please come," the Lord of the feast whispers. "There is nothing that disqualifies you from attending this celebration. Come just as you are. Sit with Me. You are welcome here."

Grace is an invitation to come as you are. Grace is the promise that there is still room. Grace is radical generosity. Grace is the healing and restoring that is abundant in Christ. Grace is a place at the table.

He extends His grace the same way He extends an invitation to His feast, no matter how broken you feel—He wants to heal you.

So we gather 'round the table, and light spills in through the windows, and we are all together.

And everyone is welcome here.

"FOR BY GRACE ARE YE SAVED THROUGH FAITH;
AND THAT NOT OF YOURSELVES:
IT IS THE GIFT OF GOD."

—EPHESIANS 2:8

chapter two

The Grace Giver

The small classroom is bursting with fourteen-year-olds. Loud conversation fills every space of the room, chairs tipped back, young people laughing. "Where were you last night?" I hear them catching up, and filling in, and the momentum carries through the door and down the hall and it reaches me before I even walk in. I have come to talk about Jesus with these boundary-pushers and insight-seekers, and I know the discussion will be intriguing before it even begins.

I hand out plain white pieces of paper, I assign partners, I ask them to draw what they know. It's because I am a visual learner—I want to see it with circles and arrows, these descriptions of life, death, judgment, and paradise. I want them to draw this plan just the way they have been taught over and over these fourteen years. They will know what to do. I don't ask them to think outside of the box. "It will be easy," I tell them. "Just draw what you know."

There is something about fourteen that is unexpected. Someone should remind you of that when you are making lesson plans for

Sunday School. I saw it when everyone placed their drawings on the floor. One stood out as a stark contrast against the rest.

It changed the direction of the lesson.

That paper changed my view of the plan.

I can't get it out of my mind. I drive home that afternoon and can't stop thinking about it. On Monday I am still pondering what happened. By Tuesday, when I still can't forget the lesson, I decide I should return to the church to get the pictures those fourteen-year-olds had drawn out of the classroom garbage bin so I will always remember. I call the bishop to ask if I can borrow his keys. "You know those papers won't still be in that room, right?" he asks me, concerned that I have lost something of great importance. "All of the garbage cans get emptied into the outside dumpster right after church."

I don't normally climb into dumpsters, but those papers *are* of great importance to me. *I have to have them.* I make my way out to my garage, keys in hand. I grab the rake, and a shovel, and a ladder, because I don't want to get permanently stuck in the dumpster behind the church. I think to myself how ridiculous this is, but still I go. I am dead set on finding those papers. When I arrive, I check the dumpster for small, gray moving animals before I get in, hovering there on the brown metal edge, gathering courage, trying to grasp hold of my brave. Then I jump in, and I am knee-deep in garbage, and I begin tearing open black plastic bags. It is in the third full bag that I find them. Seven pieces of white paper folded in half.

I climb out of the dumpster, get into the warmth of my car, and spread the papers out on the dashboard to make sure they are all there. Sure enough, they are, and the lesson I find on that one paper is still just as powerful now as it had been on Sunday.

Six of the papers have the drawings you would imagine if someone asked you to draw out the plan of salvation—circles, and arrows, and life, and death. The premortal existence and paradise. You know. *You know.* But one paper has just one word, written in bold black letters across the blank white paper: JESUS.

God's plan. From the very beginning. The thought of it still captures my heart. *Just Jesus.* Healing for ashes. Hope over hurt. Strength in weakness. The Answer. The Finisher.

JESUS.

God's plan for getting us home.

You wonder exactly how that plan works, and it is what I wonder too. And each of those fourteen-year-old hearts? It's the exact question they were asking. Because mortality brings moments of desperation, lonely places, and trials with the potential to destroy us. There are times when we hit rock bottom regardless of what we are doing to avoid the dark places. It is true; sometimes the dark places just come. Suddenly you fear your faith isn't deep enough for this world breaking apart, this struggle against the hurt that has somehow become your life.

We long for peace, a way out, a promise, an end in sight, until, unexpectedly, the light finally breaks through, shattering the darkness of the place we think we will never recover from. That light is Jesus. He enters our stories with love, and hope, and grace. We

JESUS

understand love, we cling to hope, but we often find ourselves wondering about grace. Here is an important truth—no one who undertakes a journey to understand grace is on their own. It isn't how the journey works. When we are lost, He comes to find us. When we are broken, He means to make us whole. When all is darkness, He brings life-giving light. He is the Grace Giver—and His is a journey that transforms lives, and changes hearts, and heals. *He wants to heal you.*

If we really want to understand grace, it is imperative for us to understand Jesus Christ—who He is, what He does, and why He does it. And that understanding begins in a garden. It is a garden you are familiar with, a story you have heard over and over again. If I gave you a white piece of paper you could draw it out—two trees, and a serpent, and a piece of fruit. But, for just a moment, I want you to set aside what you know about Adam and Eve, the partaking of the fruit, and the choice made in Eden, and simply picture in your head the most beautiful garden you have ever walked through.

. . .

The sun rises over the highest leaves and filters through to the soft, downy grass. Blossoms and fruit fill the air with sweet fragrance. The gentle rhythm of a flowing stream brings peace and the promise of life. I read between the lines, imagine the beauty, and learn about the tree in the midst of the garden; its gift is to make one wise. I pull out a white piece of paper, and there on the left I draw the tree. I learn that partaking of the fruit of this tree will cause one to be cut off from the presence of God. It is important.

cut off from the presence of God

tree of knowledge
of good and evil

I write it down on the paper, just above the leaves on my tree. I wonder at the significance of the truth I just wrote—*cut off from the presence of God.* I realize that means the fruit of this tree opens the door to mortality. I write that word in the middle of the tree. I realize one piece of fruit with the word *mortality* is not sufficient to describe the fruit of this tree, so I begin drawing fruit hanging from each branch and I label each piece with what I know mortality brings—death, pain, sickness, weakness, cancer, addiction, and other battles we will face here. But there is also the bearing of children, the learning, and the experiencing of joy—I must remember that. I write it all down. I know the name of the tree; it is the tree of knowledge of good and evil. I label the tree by writing the name at its base.

This is the tree that opened the way for each of us to come to earth. Remember the courageous choice Eve made in Eden? It wasn't about eating a piece of fruit. This was the choice to come to mortality, to leave the presence of God for a time, to learn wisdom, to become. There were lessons that could not be learned in heaven. Some wisdom can come only from separation. Leaving creates a longing for home that compels us to become and to return, but the Father knew we would not be able to accomplish the becoming or the returning on our own.

I can't help but think of Eve, standing there on the edge, gathering courage, trying to grasp hold of her brave. Did she know her choice would bring death, and sickness, and children, and thorns, and all of the blessings and trials that come with a life on Earth?

the tree of life

Did she know about the chance for wandering, for visiting the dark places, for experiencing the ache of discouragement? Did she understand about the separation from God? If so, it would have been frightening to consider the reality of walking away from God, knowing that her own merits would never be enough to get her back home to Him again. But God had a plan.

There was a second tree.

A tree with fruit that could overcome weakness, every dark place and each discouraging ache. A fruit that would enable us to do what we wouldn't be able to do if left to our own means. Fruit with the power to bring the wanderer home.

It is general conference in the fall of 2014. The leaves on the trees outside my home have started turning. The peach harvest has just ended, and our home is full to overflowing with fruit. It is Sunday afternoon, and the last speaker stands up and begins speaking about fruit and trees and God's love. I listen to the talk, and I begin to draw the second tree on the right side of my piece of paper. As he always does, Elder David A. Bednar begins describing a gospel principle in a way I can visualize. He explains that this tree, the tree of life, represents Jesus—His ministry, atoning sacrifice, and Resurrection. He teaches us that the fruit of this tree can be considered a symbol for the blessings that come through the Savior's Atonement. I write *Jesus* in the middle of the tree. I could write *Atonement* next to one piece of fruit, but I don't. I begin drawing fruit hanging from each branch, and I label each piece with the blessings Christ's Atonement brings—there is eternal life,

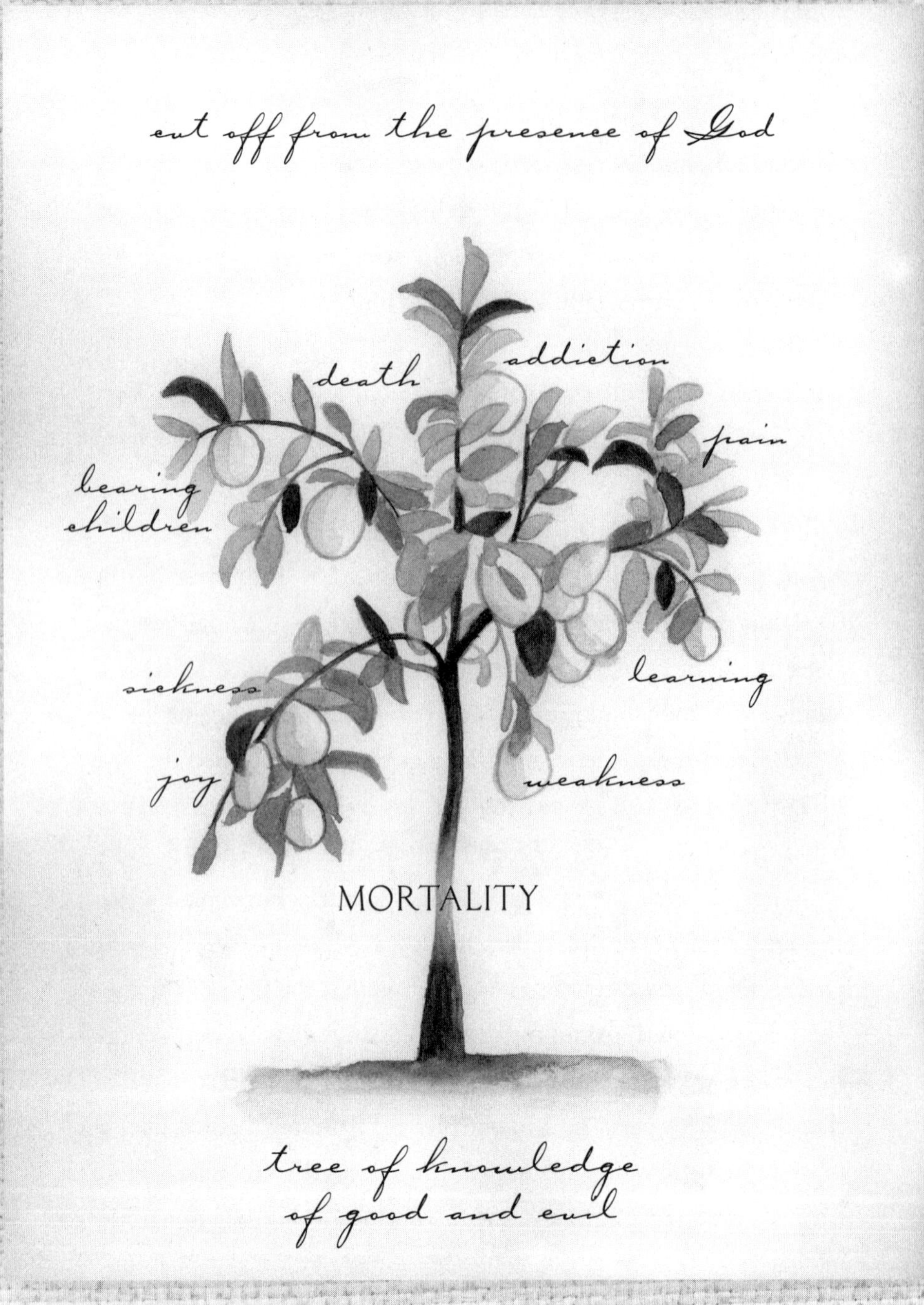
cut off from the presence of God
death
addiction
pain
bearing children
sickness
learning
joy
weakness
MORTALITY
tree of knowledge of good and evil

return to the presence of God

the tree of life

love, healing, peace, hope, and strength. I write down *covenants* and *grace.* I know the name of this tree—it is the tree of life. I label the tree by writing the name at its base. This tree has the power to bring us back into the presence of God, to counter every hard thing mortality brings. It is an important truth. I write it down on the paper, just above the leaves on my tree.

I look at the two trees on my paper and understanding comes. The tree of knowledge of good and evil represents mortality. The Father knew we needed to experience mortality in order to progress. Mortality included lessons that couldn't be learned in heaven. There were trials and tests and testimonies that could only be experienced on earth. But He didn't mean for us to take that journey alone. The second tree becomes the key. God sent us a Savior. Jesus. He would walk with us along the way. Through the power of His grace, the Savior would enable us to overcome everything mortality would bring.

We must remember that.

I have come to believe God doesn't give us cancer, or Down Syndrome, or blindness, or anxiety and depression; *mortality does.* Entering mortality means biological factors, cells that could mutate, and illnesses or addictions that could cause harm. It means loved ones will die. It means accidents, and poor choices, and struggles that could leave us wounded.

We chose mortality fully knowing God would *allow* mortality to do its work in us, even though that work would be painful. We also knew that engaging in and overcoming these trials of mortality with Him would transform us to become more like Him. His gift of grace is what allows that transformation to take place.

I glance down at my paper again and more understanding comes; the trees really do stand in opposition to each other. For every hurt on the mortality tree, healing can be found on the Jesus tree. The one becomes the answer for the other. I begin to understand. The Father knew that mortality would be a hard and heart-wrenching journey, but He didn't leave us to walk through it alone. We must remember that there was more than just two significant trees in that first garden; there was also a plan.

JESUS.

The Father planned a rescue. He knew what it would take to find the one who is lost. The walking into the mountains, the searching through the wilderness places. He knew the only way back for each of us from this mortal experience, the only way back to the presence of God, would require a Savior that was willing to come from heaven to mortality, into the lost places. A Deliverer who would extend the enabling grace that would make it possible for us to return; a Redeemer who would take our hand and lead the way back home, no matter how far we had wandered.

. . .

I open the Book of Mormon and begin to read the story of this Savior coming down, this rescue planned from the beginning. I want to know the details, to understand them. "*Lord, how is it done?*" (Enos 1:7; emphasis added). In the eleventh chapter of First Nephi, the angel calls it condescension, but Nephi calls it love (see

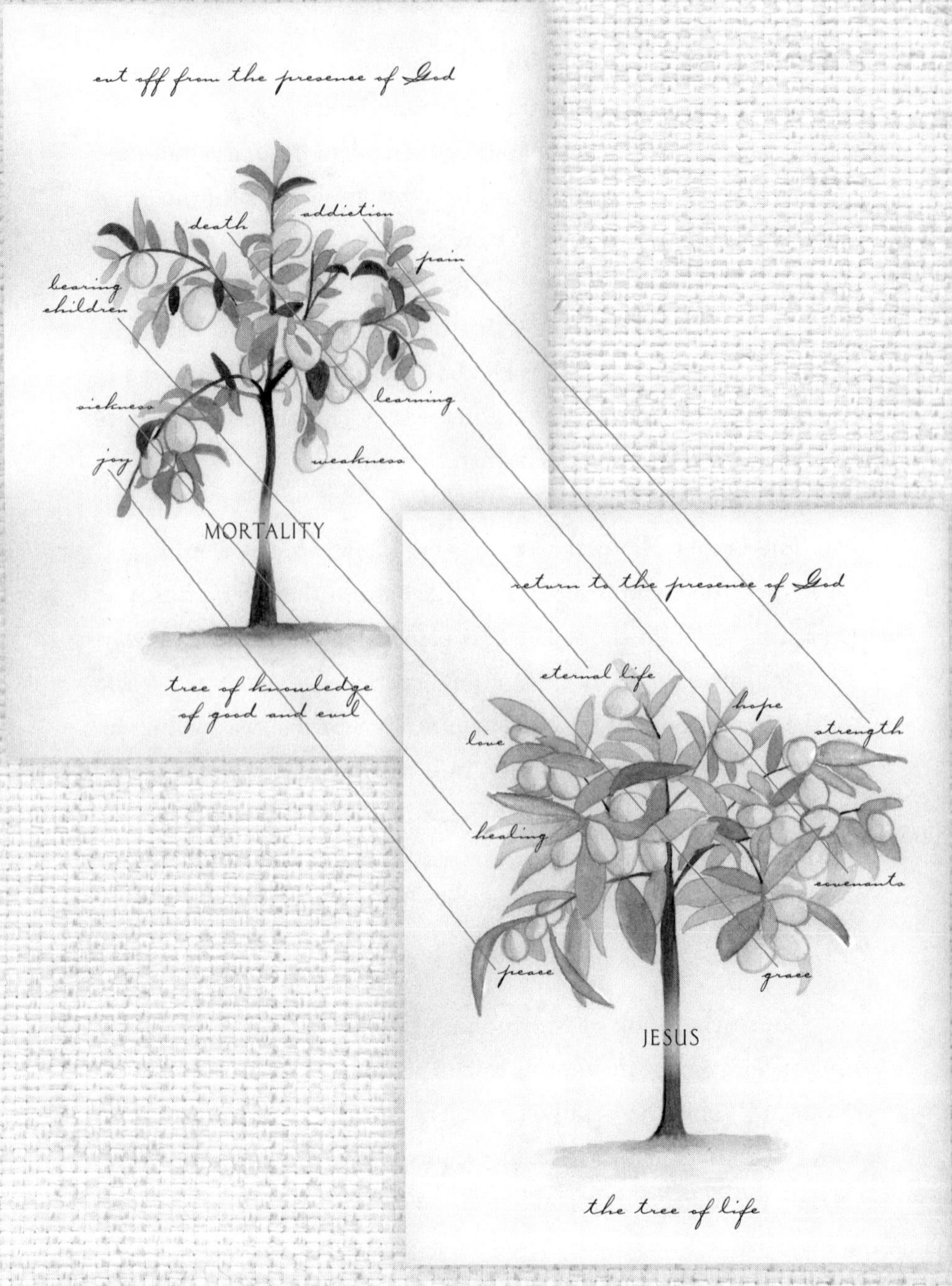
cut off from the presence of God
death
addiction
pain
bearing children
learning
sickness
joy
weakness
MORTALITY
tree of knowledge of good and evil
return to the presence of God
eternal life
hope
strength
love
healing
covenants
peace
grace
JESUS
the tree of life

1 Nephi 11:16, 22). I want to understand more about this condescension called love, about the reality of a love so strong it would compel a Savior to descend to the level of His followers in order to provide a rescue. To come into the darkest places and the deepest hurts in order to lift each one of us. To extend to each of us His enabling grace.

The Spirit first asks Nephi a question beginning with two words, "Believest thou . . . ?" and Nephi answers, "Yea, thou knowest that I believe. . . ." To which the Spirit replies, "Because thou believest . . . thou shalt behold the things which thou hast desired" (1 Nephi 11:4-6), *and maybe we underestimate the importance of belief.*

So Nephi believes, and the angel begins.

I love this angel because instead of giving Nephi a wordy definition, he describes God's love, this condescension, with three different scenes. I am a visual learner; I too learn best when I see it all laid out before me. I want to create a picture of each of these scenes, so I pull out another white piece of paper, and I begin to draw.

"Look," the angel says, and Nephi sees the city of Nazareth, and there within the city a young woman who is about to become a mother. The angel asks an important question: "Knowest thou the condescension of God?" (1 Nephi 11:16). I pause to look up the word *condescend*; I want to understand what it means. The definition is simple—to come down with. I think of a baby coming down into the poorest of circumstance, into the lowest of places, where He would grow and learn and come to understand grace for grace.

he came down

I draw the stable and the mother and the tiny baby and consider what I have learned. Condescension began in a humble stable under a starry sky, in the moment when Jesus Christ came down to earth to meet His people where they were. I finish drawing the first picture and turn back to the story again.

"Look," the angel says, "and behold the condescension of God!" (1 Nephi 11:26). As I read, I begin to draw again. This time condescension is shown as the Redeemer of the world is baptized. I see how He entered into the same covenant His people would, to mourn with those that mourn, comfort those that stand in need of comfort, and bear another's burden. The next verses show how He went forth living that covenant, ministering to all—those who were sick and who were afflicted. I read how they were healed by the power of the Lamb. I draw pictures of the Lord visiting us in our very worst moments, in our lowest places, and bringing healing to us there. This is condescension, I remind myself. This is a Savior offering grace where we are. I finish drawing the second picture and turn back to the story again.

"Look," the angel says again, and I begin to draw. Now the Son of the everlasting God is judged according to the ways of the world; He is lifted up on the cross, slain in a manner befitting the least of all citizens. He died the lowest death. I finish the picture and realize condescension, love, is a Savior who agreed to descend below them all in order to make certain He could bring them all back home.

I lay out all of my pictures and I realize *this* is love, *this* is condescension—the birth, the healing ministry, and the atoning sacrifice

to heal us

of Jesus Christ. This is a Brother willing to rescue His family. This is a Rescuer intent on walking up every mountain and through any wilderness in order to find every lost one. A Deliverer who meets you in your lowest places in order to bring you home. The invitation to His table, the Father's plan, the two trees in the garden, and the condescension are all witnesses of His grace. In the margin of my scriptures, right next to 1 Nephi 11:16, where the angel asks, "Knowest thou the condescension of God?" I have one phrase written: Condescension—the ability of God to come to our level.

To bring His grace to where we are.

. . .

It is late afternoon when I receive the text from my good friend Kris, who is blind.

"Come sit with me. Come talk to me about Jesus."

She has just come home from the hospital. There was a twelve-and-a-half-hour surgery, and time in the ICU, and we are fighting the battle of cancer again. I say "we" because we all feel the pain of it, but she is the one who bears the wounds. This is her tree, the fruit of her mortal journey, and she longs for the reminder of Christ who heals.

On Sunday it will be Easter, and she asks me to tell her what I have been studying. My thoughts fill up with Jesus. I remind her how I am fascinated by the stories in which Jesus meets people where they are. We talk about the woman at her well and Peter in the water. We talk about the lame man at his pool, the blind man with his parents, and the daughter of Jairus in her bedroom. There is the woman in her moment of shame, the leper in his colony, and the man in the Gadarenes. We recount all the stories we can think of. We are reminded that this is the pattern of Jesus, the message of His life. He meets us where we are.

"I found one more," I tell her. "It is a tender one. My favorite discovery of Easter. The best of my study so far." She wonders if there could be a best. "Remember the criminal?" I ask her. "Jesus met him on his cross."

The realization takes her breath away.

We try to consider what this means. In the very last moments of His mortality, in the midst of His own excruciating pain, Jesus was still living out His mission of condescension. Meeting people where they were, as they were. Even on the cross. We sit for a minute in silence to think about this.

"Don't just teach people that He met them where they were," she whispers. I look over at her as she gathers her thoughts. Her eyes are bandaged in gauze, there are stitches holding together the fresh wounds on her cheeks and down her lip. I see the staples holding the tender skin of her shoulder where the lymph nodes have been removed. She breathes slowly, taking a break from the oxygen mask that is beside her bed. "You need to teach them that He descended lower than us all. Lower than the pain we will ever suffer. So He can lift us."

It is the promise of a Savior who said, "My Father sent me that I might be lifted up upon the cross; and after that I had been lifted

in our lowest places

up upon the cross, that I might draw all men unto me" (3 Nephi 27:14).

All men.

Every one of us.

Even the criminal on his cross.

"NEVERTHELESS, THE LORD GOD
SHOWETH US OUR WEAKNESS
THAT WE MAY KNOW THAT IT IS BY HIS GRACE,
AND HIS GREAT CONDESCENSIONS
UNTO THE CHILDREN OF MEN,
THAT WE HAVE POWER TO DO THESE THINGS."

—JACOB 4:7

chapter three

GRACE WHERE YOU ARE

The blossoms are in full bloom. I can see them through the window; their fragrance passes through the back door that had been propped open, allowing a gentle breeze to fill the room. We sit in the family room talking—me, Meg, and Meg's best friend, Sam. The girls are grown up now. Sam holds her own little one on her lap. We are talking about Jesus, but mostly about His grace.

Life looks different for each of us. Meg is taking twenty-one credits in college; she is trying to balance her classes and homework with all the rest of her life. Sam's mornings are spent at hair school, and her afternoons and evenings are filled with caring for her husband and new baby daughter. They are both happy, but I can tell they are stretched thin—both doing their best in the places where they are. I remember those days. The moments when you felt like you weren't enough for everything that had been placed in front of you. I smile a little as the truth dawns on me. I am two decades older than they are, my kids are gone, my college days are over, and

I still feel like I'm not enough for everything that has been placed in front of me. *And maybe we never are enough.*

It's why we are talking about grace. How His grace is made perfect in our weakness (see 2 Corinthians 12:9). How that grace can make up the difference. We wonder if it is possible for someone to live in grace daily. *Do you ever wonder what that would look like?*

"I just don't understand it," Sam says, Meg nodding her head in agreement. "I feel like you have to DO something in order to experience grace."

I know what she is talking about. It is the line in 2 Nephi 25:23: "By grace . . . we are saved, after all we can do." I nod my understanding.

"It just doesn't make sense to me," she says with a question in her eyes, in her heart. She is intent. "I've spent my entire adult life trying to figure out what I am supposed to DO."

I look at these two girls who don't have time in their schedules to DO anything more than they are already doing. I can feel their worry and inadequacy; I feel that same weight. I know exactly what they are asking. *What more would they need to do in order to qualify for grace?* It is a question I have asked myself many times. A question that has sent me time after time back into the scriptures, because I can think of several scripture stories where the people didn't DO anything, and yet somehow, they still received grace.

I tell the girls that. "Can you think of stories from the scriptures where a person received grace without having to DO something?" I ask.

We pull out a white piece of paper and start making a list.

a list of stories...

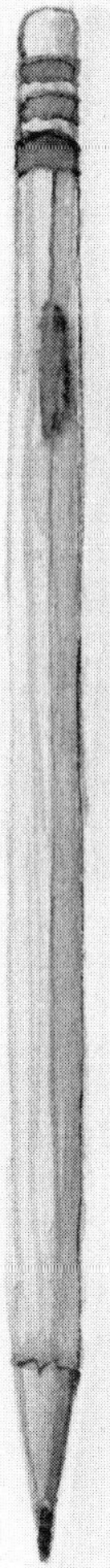

The First Story: Caught

The columns of the temple stand tall. Immovable. Their shade spills over the corner of the courtyard. Our group has gathered in the reprieve of the shade, waiting for the teaching to begin.

The hot sun beats down, baking the dirt and the stones and the skin. Relentless. I stand at the edge of the shade, there in the temple courtyard of the Bible video set in Goshen, Utah, waiting with all of the religious educators who have gathered there. Finally, one of the Bible teachers moves to the front of the group and begins to speak. He asks for a volunteer as his eyes scan over the gathered crowd, and then they settle on me. He gestures with his hand, an invitation. *Come.* So, I walk up to the front, out of the protection of the shade, into the blazing sun. "I need you to settle yourself on the ground," he says, "as if you've been thrown there by angry hands. I don't want you to be comfortable."

I settle into the dusty floor of the courtyard, realizing I have just been pulled into the scripture story as he begins to read.

"'Early in the morning he came again into the temple, and all the people came unto him; and he sat down, and taught them. And the scribes and Pharisees brought unto him a woman taken in adultery; and when they had set her in the midst . . .'"

As I listen, my eyes focus on the man who is reading the story. He doesn't just stand still in front of the group as he reads; instead he stands up and stoops down, as the story says.

"'They say unto him, Master, this woman was taken in adultery, in the very act. Now Moses in the law commanded us, that such should be stoned: but what sayest thou? This they said, tempting him, that they might have to accuse him. *But Jesus stooped down*, and with his finger wrote on the ground.'"

As he reads, the teacher bends down and puts his finger in the dust, right next to where I am. There is silence for a few seconds as he draws, and then he begins to read again.

"'So when they continued asking him, *he lifted up himself*, and said unto them, He that is without sin among you, let him first cast a stone at her. And again *he stooped down*, and wrote on the ground. And they which heard it, being convicted by their own conscience, went out one by one, beginning at the eldest, even unto the last: and Jesus was left alone, and the woman *standing* in the midst'" (John 8:2–9; emphasis added).

The reading stops, and the teacher looks at me. He is still crouched down, waiting. But what is he waiting for? I think back over the last words he read and realize the woman was no longer supposed to be lying in the dirt. So I stand up and begin brushing myself off.

"'When Jesus had *lifted up himself*,'" he continued, rising up to stand beside me, "'he said unto her, Woman, where are those thine accusers? hath no man condemned thee?

"'She said, No man, Lord. And Jesus said unto her, Neither do I condemn thee: go, and sin no more'" (vv. 10–11).

There is silence. The teacher closes his Bible and then looks at me with careful eyes. "Now," he says, as if he and I are the only two people in the courtyard, "what did you learn?"

The lesson is clear. It doesn't come from the words that were spoken; it comes from the actions that had been demonstrated. The stooping down and the lifting up. Jesus met the woman caught in adultery at her level. *He met her where she was.* There, in the middle of a temple courtyard, He extended His grace. Grace in the form of forgiveness. Grace in invitation to a new way of life.

grace where she was.

Questions start running through my mind. *What had this woman done to qualify for grace?* She had been caught in the very act. *What was her "all she could do"?* None of it made sense, and yet, clearly, His grace had been extended.

The Second Story: Threatened

The road where the Lord met Saul consisted of more than just dirt. It harbored the marks of a man on the road to Damascus. A man breathing out threatenings and slaughter. A man with a letter in hand that gave permission for him to bring the men and women of Christ bound to Jerusalem. This was a man intent on persecuting the Church, the people, and the Lord.

And yet, there in that threatening place, light shone down from heaven, and the Lord spoke, and that man was given a second chance. Saul was extended grace many would say was undeserved—an invitation and encouragement to change through the enabling power of Jesus Christ.

It was three days later when the Lord visited Ananias. "Go . . . and inquire . . . for one called Saul" (Acts 9:11).

Ananias couldn't help but wonder why. He had heard of Saul. The man was filled with hatred, with the intent to destroy; he was capable of great harm. *Do you know who this man is?* he questioned the Lord.

It is the Lord's response that captures my thoughts: "Go thy way: for he is a chosen vessel unto me" (Acts 9:15).

This man who carried a letter in hand to bind the Saints, the man breathing out threatenings and slaughter, who was intent on persecuting the Church, was chosen? Every time I read those verses it is as confusing to me as it must have been for Ananias.

For some reason the Lord saw through the threatenings, the slaughter, the persecution, and still He extended grace.

grace as he was.

Why?

Again, questions start running through my mind. *What had Saul done to qualify for grace in that moment?* He had been caught in the very act. *What was his "all you can do"?* None of it made sense, and yet, clearly, grace had been extended.

The Third Story: Unbelieving

I can't help but wonder what condition the father's heart was in when he approached the Lord that day. The burden of caring for his son had surely worn him through. It had been years of pulling the child away from burning flames and out of water that could easily drown him. The weight and the worry must have been evident in his eyes, in his heart, in the way his shoulders sagged down with the burden that consumed his life.

"If thou canst do anything," he pled with the Savior, "have compassion on us, and help us."

"Jesus said unto him, If thou canst believe, all things are possible to him that believeth" (Mark 9:22–23).

I read the scripture and I notice the same thing every time: the Savior asked one thing of the father. There was only one requirement for the healing to take place: *believe.*

And yet, even that simple request was more than the father was capable of. "And straightway the father of the child cried out, and said with tears, Lord, I believe; help thou mine unbelief" (Mark 9:24).

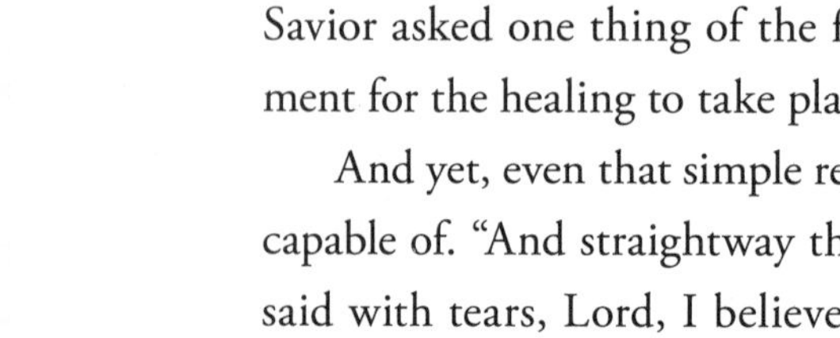

The Lord saw the broken father, saw his doubt, saw his unbelief, and still He extended grace. *Even though the father could not completely live up to the only request the Savior had given.*

Even when his "after all" was not enough. None of it made sense, and yet, clearly, grace had been extended.

. . .

After adding these three stories to our list, the girls and I come to a conclusion: These three people didn't *have* to do anything. Grace was extended exactly where they were and exactly as they were. The truth of it settles softly into our conversation—the Lord will meet you where you are, as you are, but another truth quickly follows—He doesn't intend to leave you there. "'Come as you are,' a loving Father says to each of us, but He adds: 'Don't plan to stay as you are'" (Jeffrey R. Holland, "Songs Sung and Unsung", *Ensign*, May 2017). We find comfort in knowing we can come as we are with the understanding that His grace, continually offered no matter the condition we are in, has the power to lift us, heal us, and enable us to grow and change from exactly where we are in our stories to a fullness of life through Him.

It isn't long before we realize it wasn't just these three people who experienced the grace of the Lord in a very personal way—the more we search through stories, the more witnesses we find. Each of those witnesses becomes a chapter, and the chapters fill up books, and the books are bound together in what we know as scripture. And maybe that is what scripture is, a testament or witness of grace—individual stories explaining how the Lord met people where they were, how He interacted with His people on a very personal and intimate level in those places, and how He lifted them through grace to a fuller life.

. . .

It is after we lay out each of these stories on paper that the girls' question resurfaces. They both recognize how grace worked in the stories we had found, but it still doesn't bridge the gap. "I can see what you are talking about," Meg says, "but I still feel like I have to DO something. If what you are saying is true, then what does 'after all we can do' really mean?"

It is a good question. We decide that the best expert on the subject would probably be the very man who delivered the sermon itself, Nephi. We open the scriptures again. This time, instead of focusing on that one verse, which is what we had always previously done, the girls and I turn to the whole chapter of 2 Nephi 25 to see what we can learn from Nephi's entire message.

Maybe you are like Meg and Sam. Maybe you have always wondered about the "after all we can do." If so, let's take a minute to study Nephi's sermon. There is learning there that is important. If you pull out a piece of paper, if you grab a pen and start reading in verse 16, and read on until you get to verse 29, you will begin to see a pattern start to develop. Watch for the one phrase Nephi repeats over and over again in chapter 25, and it isn't "after all we can do." Instead it is a call to action, a call that becomes our *all we can do*. The two girls and I begin to read, and every time we find the familiar phrase repeated time and time again throughout these verses, we write it down. Maybe you could too.

- They shall be persuaded to *believe in Christ*, the Son of God, and the Atonement (v. 16).

believe in Christ

- That day shall come that they shall *believe in Christ* (v. 16)
- We labor diligently to write, to persuade our children, and also our brethren, to *believe in Christ* (v. 23).
- We *believe in Christ* (v. 24).
- For the right way is *to believe in Christ* and deny him not (v. 28).
- And now behold, I say unto you that the right way is to *believe in Christ* (v. 29).

Nephi makes it really clear: "For we labor diligently to write, to persuade our children, and also our brethren, to *believe in Christ*, and to be reconciled to God; for we know that it is by grace that we are saved, after all we can do" (2 Nephi 25:23; emphasis added). And what if Nephi is saying *all you can do* is *believe in Christ*? What if we have been overemphasizing the wrong line in verse 23 and missing something just as important? What if the most important line isn't *all we can do*; what if the most important line in that verse is *believe in Christ*? It is a truth that makes sense to all three of us, especially after reading each of the scripture stories we have found—grace is not about what *we* can do; it's all about what *He* can do. And maybe it makes sense to you.

Dieter F. Uchtdorf said, "I wonder if sometimes we misinterpret the phrase 'after all we can do.' We must understand that 'after' does not equal 'because.' We are not saved 'because' of all that we can do. Have any of us done all that we can do? Does God wait until we've expended every effort before He will intervene in our lives with His saving grace?

"I am certain Nephi knew that the Savior's grace allows and enables us to overcome sin. That is why Nephi labored so diligently to persuade his children and brethren to *believe in Christ*, and to be reconciled to God. After all, *that is* what we can do!" ("The Gift of Grace," *Ensign*, May 2015; emphasis added).

. . .

The girls finish reading and decide it can't be true. It's too easy. *All we have to do is believe in Christ?* "Well, we have two witnesses," I tell them. "There has to be truth here. So, what is the next question we should be asking?" It dawns on all three of us at the same time:

If we are saved by grace
after all we can do,
and all we can do is
believe in Christ,
what, then, does it mean
to believe?

chapter four

The Power of Belief

He set a goal to cross Niagara Falls on a tightrope. Unthinkable. Impossible. The planning was intense. No one thought it could be done. It was a feat that had never been accomplished before. But Charles Blondin was determined to make the crossing.

I'm not sure how he did it, how he stretched that 1,100-foot rope from the Canadian border clear across to the United States and anchored it on both sides. I read about how the guylines were attached every twenty feet onto the thick rope stretched taut 160 feet above the water, hoping to offset the gusts coming over the falls, and I cannot even begin to fathom how it was done.

Hundreds of people came to examine the rope, to determine the safety of the attempt, to give their opinion on whether or not the crossing could be completed. They all said the same thing: Blondin would not be able to accomplish the journey because the rope would not be capable of sustaining him. But Blondin wasn't deterred.

On June 30, 1859, with 25,000 people watching, Charles

Blondin took one step and then another onto the mist-covered rope. He leaned into the wind coming off of the falls.

Unbelievably, he made it all the way across.

Once he had accomplished that first journey, Blondin was ready to attempt it again. He started working toward his next crossing, and after that one, the next. Charles Blondin crossed Niagara Falls over three hundred times in his lifetime, and almost every time he did something different. Once he crossed blindfolded; another time he crossed on stilts. On July 4, he took an old-fashioned camera across the rope, stopped in the middle, put the black cloth over his head and took a photo of the crowd, and then continued his journey. Another time he crossed the rope with a potato sack over his head.

On July 15, Blondin walked backward on the tightrope one step at a time to Canada and then returned to the United States pushing a small, metal wheelbarrow. The crowd cheered as he stepped off of the rope and onto the safety of the soil. Then he yelled into the crowd, "Do you believe I can carry a person across the rope in this wheelbarrow?"

The crowd enthusiastically yelled, "Yes! You are the greatest tightrope walker in the world. We believe you can!"

"Okay," said Blondin, looking carefully over the group, "who wants to get into the wheelbarrow?"

No one did.

I can't help but think to myself every time I hear this story, *What if someone had? What would have been the difference between the crowd and a person who would get in the wheelbarrow?*

believe

Always, just one word comes to mind.

Belief.

And for the two girls sitting on the couch in my family room, the thought of believing in Christ is almost as hard as climbing into that wheelbarrow. It will require testing His promises, trusting that He really will follow through. It means we have to believe that He will meet us where we are and then take us to places we wouldn't be able to get to on our own. Through His grace.

The girls and I pull out another white piece of paper and prepare to write.

"When it comes to grace, what does He say He will do?" I ask, pulling my leather-bound scriptures closer and opening their familiar pages. What is it, exactly, that we are supposed to believe? We start searching for the word *grace.*

And then, we begin to write down every scripture we can find.

"AND NOW . . . I COMMEND YOU TO GOD, AND TO THE WORD OF HIS GRACE, WHICH IS ABLE TO BUILD YOU UP."

—ACTS 20:32

PART TWO

believe in Christ

chapter five

My Grace Will Deliver and Preserve You

"AND BEHOLD HOW GREAT THE COVENANTS OF THE LORD, AND HOW GREAT HIS CONDESCENSIONS UNTO THE CHILDREN OF MEN; AND BECAUSE OF HIS GREATNESS, AND HIS GRACE AND MERCY, HE HAS PROMISED UNTO US THAT OUR SEED SHALL NOT UTTERLY BE DESTROYED . . . BUT THAT HE WOULD PRESERVE THEM."

—2 NEPHI 9:53

Sometimes the only way home when you are lost is for someone to come take your hand and lead you there. Just like the boy who wandered off in the West Desert near Delta, Utah, when he was three years old. He tried to find his way back, tried calling out the names of his grandpa, his dad, and his brothers, tried to remember where everyone had been. The day was the hottest on record for that time of the year, but the night would bring strong south winds signaling the approach of a late spring storm. Snow was forecast, the temperature was dropping, and the conditions were terrible for a three-year-old wandering through the wilderness alone. He didn't know about staying warm, about finding shelter, about the need for water. He just knew he was all tired out. So, that night after walking and walking as far as he could go, the tiny boy with his blistered sunburn sat down next to a rock to wait.

They called in the search and rescue, they called in the army, they called in every friend and family member they knew. By nightfall over five hundred rescuers were combing the desert in search of the three-year-old boy, but he was not found that night. It was hours and hours later, after the night had ended and morning had come, after prayers had been cried out, and rescuers had searched the terrain, after airplanes and K-9 teams and search and rescue had looked for almost thirty-six hours, when one man showed up on the scene.

He had come home late from work that day and missed the ride with those who had left for the rescue hours before. He almost didn't go. But, when he got home, his wife had packed the car with a sleeping bag, some water, and a flashlight, so he drove down to the West Desert alone. When he got to the command table everyone else was already out searching. Not knowing where to go, he knelt down to pray and then he started to walk. He hiked through the valley and up the dunes and started up the steep side of a mountain. After he had walked for hours, his inclination told him this terrain was too rough for a three-year-old to navigate, the trail too steep. Reason told him that it was too far from the base camp, but the Spirit urged him on. Three other groups had gotten that far earlier in the day; they had been on that same trail, had struggled against the same terrain, had reached that exact same location, and all of them had turned back for home. But this man kept walking through the loose shale, up the steep path, and along the top of the mountain until he finally found the three-year-old boy waiting patiently next to the rock.

For a rescue.

For a way back.

He just wanted to go home.

That three-year-old boy just needed someone to meet him where he was, as he was, and then take him to the place he wasn't capable of getting to on his own.

And aren't we all waiting for a rescue?

For a way back?

Don't we all want to go home?

. . .

It is Thursday afternoon and I have just finished teaching a lesson on grace to a group of women in my neighborhood church building. Out of the corner of my eye, I see her raise her hand, the older woman who sits with her scriptures open on her lap. I notice how her soft, white hair frames her gentle face, how her piercing blue eyes question. "I don't understand what you are saying. Do you believe everyone will be saved? Also, what do you mean by salvation? And what do you mean by belief?" I recognize the processing taking place within her heart, this struggling to understand grace.

Even though the lesson is over, we address the question we haven't yet explored from a verse found in the second chapter of

Philippians: "Wherefore, my beloved, as ye have always obeyed, not as in my presence only, but now much more in my absence, *work out your own salvation* with fear and trembling" (Philippians 2:12; emphasis added).

The woman with her scriptures on her lap wants to know where the working out of our own salvation fits with what Nephi taught about believing in Christ. They are good questions. I add one more. I ask her why we would need a rescue, or a deliverer, if we could work out our way back home on our own. It is a conundrum. In order to grasp a deeper understanding of this, we look up the Greek translation for the word "work," and the word "salvation."

The Greek word for "work" is *katergazomai*; it means "to finish or accomplish." "Salvation" comes from the Greek word *sozo,* which means "to rescue, to deliver, to heal, and to save." We discuss these words for a minute and then I ask a question. "How many of us can do that on our own? Which of you is prepared to *finish or accomplish* mortality? How many of you can rescue yourself when you have wandered off, can deliver yourself out of a wilderness place, or can heal yourself from that which has weakened you? Could you *work that out* alone?"

I watch the women slowly begin shaking their heads.

It is silent for a time as we ponder this.

I think of the three-year-old boy sitting against the rock in the West Desert, Saul on the road to Damascus, the woman caught in adultery, the father who struggled with unbelief, and even my daughter and her friend Sam. Which of those are left to work out their own saving? Are any of them in charge of their own deliverance? What if that three-year-old's only option was to work out his own way back home?

After a moment of considering, we read the next verse: "For it is God which *worketh in you* both to will and to do of his good pleasure" (Philippians 2:13; emphasis added). In this verse, the word "worketh" is *energeo*, "to be active, be mighty in, to shew forth self." Here is the answer. We don't work out our salvation on our own—God worketh in us. It is a process of individual belief combined with divine enablement. Our belief allows Him to become active in our lives, mighty. To show forth His work in us. To bring us home.

We end the class by looking up the Hebrew translations of the word "deliver." There are two different versions of the word in the Old Testament. One is *Magan*, "to shield, to hand us safely over." The other is *Yasha*, "to succor, to defend, to help, to preserve, to rescue, to save." We consider what each of those words has to do with the character of Christ and His gift of grace.

Our Father knew the only way back for each of us from this mortal experience would require a Deliverer who was willing to come from heaven to where we were, into the lost places, extending the enabling grace that would help us get back home. He sent His Son to preserve us, to help us, to hand us safely over. One who would hike up every mountain, who would walk through the roughest terrain, who wouldn't give up or turn back until He found us. He knows we are waiting.

For a rescue.

For a way back.

For a Deliverer who is willing to bring us home.

I don't know what your story looks like right now.
Maybe you are looking for someone
to deliver and preserve you.

Christ promises,

my grace has the power to defend,
to succor, to shield,
and to hand you safely over to God.

Believe Christ.

"HOW SHALL I DELIVER THEE, ISRAEL?"

—HOSEA 11:8

chapter six

My Grace Will Help in Time of Need

"LET US THEREFORE COME BOLDLY
UNTO THE THRONE OF GRACE,
THAT WE MAY OBTAIN MERCY,
AND FIND GRACE TO HELP IN TIME OF NEED."

—HEBREWS 4:16

It is Sunday, and she stands at the front of the room with a stack of papers in her hand and her heart full of the lessons that can only be learned from a life walked intimately with God. We trust her to teach us because of the life she has lived—the valiant fight against cancer, the loss of her sight of the everyday things but not her vision of God. Yes, we trust her.

She asks us to be vulnerable, this woman who has laid out her soul to us, and so we will. Then she hands out the white pieces of paper all around the room. Little white squares passed down the rows with yellow no. 2 pencils, freshly sharpened for the writing that is about to take place.

"I want you to finish this statement with the first word that comes to mind." She gives out the instructions carefully, making sure we fully understand. "I want you to be vulnerable," she reminds us, and then she gives us the statement to complete: "Lately I have felt . . ."

And if you had been sitting there with a white piece of paper in hand, *I wonder what you would have written.*

We each finish writing, we fold our papers in half, and we pass them up to the huge silver bowl waiting in the front of the room. The woman who cannot see asks a friend to come up and read the papers from the bowl. One by one the papers are read out loud, and there are over sixty people in the room. Why did so many of us write the same word?

Overwhelmed.

Overwhelmed.

Overwhelmed.

There are other words there too. *Stressed. Tired. Inadequate. Defeated. Lacking in some respect. Discouraged. Sad. Alone. Searching. Lonely. Like I'm losing my family.* A handful of happy answers are found in the bowl, but the majority of the responses are similar to these. I think to myself how this woman who cannot see somehow has the gift to look into the souls of each of us sitting in that room. She is wise like that; she can sense how many of us would feel the same thing. I think to myself, *This is a group of women who need more than just an understanding of grace; these women need to learn what it actually means to live in grace.* And then, this dear woman begins to teach about how His grace has filled up the ordinary

lately I have felt . . .

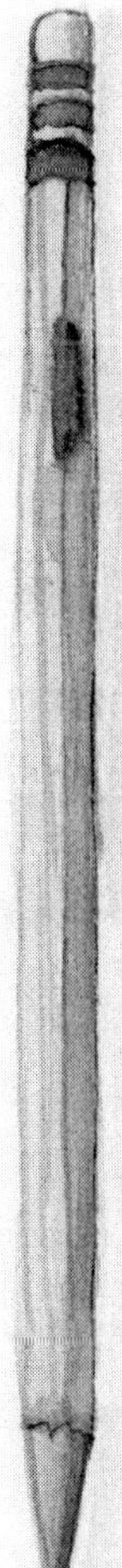

moments of her life, how she has found His grace to help in time of need.

If it were possible, I would invite you to come meet my friend Kris, who has such a beautiful vision of God and grace. It would be a summer's evening, and we would sit down on my front porch to talk about these things. My friend would ask you to describe what your story looks like, where your heart is right now. That is her way. You might say there are things that disqualify you from receiving His grace, and she would answer that those things don't matter. She would tell you the God she believes in is bigger than those things.

Maybe you are the young mother with a list that never ends. Your car is full of cleats, and McDonald's french fries, and that homework page that no one can find, but you know it's in there somewhere. You really want to be better, stronger, more capable than you are right now, but you are the soccer mom and the room mother and the neighborhood taxi, and you're tired, and worn out.

It doesn't matter how empty your reserves . . .

Maybe your heart carries devastating news—the kind that presses down and lingers ever present. You hang on to hope where there is none, and faith feels like it might disappoint, and every prayer is a pleading.

It doesn't matter how deep the dark place . . .

Maybe those decisions you made in that moment when you were so angry with God are holding you back from entering the relationship again. You worry whether He can be trusted; you worry whether you can be trusted. You worry that you might have taken one too many steps in the wrong direction, and the coming back feels harder than the staying away.

It doesn't matter how far you've wandered . . .

Maybe you feel that there isn't a place for you. You don't look like everyone else, or believe the same way everyone else does. Your life is a series of circumstances that hold you back from ever experiencing a fullness of joy. Disappointment and despair are places you have become too familiar with, and what if there are no resolutions in this life for you?

It doesn't matter how discouraging the ache . . .

You're not too far.

Everyone has a story, a need, a lack, a place of inadequacy. I know the details of mine, and you know the details of yours. And the Lord? He knows about every story, and every dark place, and every hope and heartache and happily ever after.

He sees all of them.

Perhaps He sees you trying to follow your dreams and live your best life, how you want to make a difference. He knows the desires of your heart and the imaginations of your thoughts and how you wonder if you have what it takes to succeed. His grace has the power to lift and enable you.

Maybe He sees you caving to the worry that presses in, how it wakes you, heart pounding, in the night. He knows the inner turmoil, the uneasiness, the tension that sometimes forces you to disengage, to seek solitude, to long for the peace that never comes. His grace has the power to calm and strengthen you.

He sees you waking at the break of the day to start the routine again, the feeding, the changing, the never living your own life because you are completely invested in theirs. He sees how the caregiving, the sacrifice, the serving require you to burn the midnight oil. Hands that are worn, eyes that are heavy, He sees this. His grace has the power to fill your reserves.

He sees you struggling through the addiction that chases you, that whispers to you in your idle moments, that won't loose its hold on you. How you try to be strong, how you sometimes succumb. His grace has the power to intensify and reinforce your fight.

He sees you battling memories that try to destroy you, that haunt your thoughts in the midnight hours, the traumas that won't be forgotten. He knows they have a hold over you, over your happiness, how you feel like a hostage to the past. His grace has the power to shift your focus forward so you can leave that past behind.

He sees you aching from the loss, how you mourn the memories you'll never make together, the life moments they will never see, the parts of the journey they will never know. His grace has the power to bring the healing balm of Gilead for the wounds that feel too deep.

He sees you trying to mend the rift, to understand the enlarging gap, sees you wondering how they can walk away so easily, how they don't seem to care, how their choices are breaking your family, your heart, how this is breaking you. His grace has the power to enlarge your capacity for patience, for understanding, for love.

He sees you longing for what will complete you and fearing it will never come. How you yearn for love, for companionship, to find security. How you are still walking the journey alone. His grace has the power to encircle you with love, with confidence, with peace.

He sees you trying to overcome the hurt, to let go of the injustice, to rid your soul of that which embitters you. He sees how every day you try to forgive that which seems unforgiveable. How you want to trust, to love, to believe that you have worth. His grace has the power to help you release and let go of what has been broken in you so you can begin to live again.

He sees you embarking on a journey driven by faith, but with a hint of fear. How you are entering into something unexpected that has the potential for so much good in your life, but how it will require more sacrifice than you have ever given before. His grace has the power to empower you, increase your capacity, and illuminate your view.

He sees you.

"However late you think you are, however many chances you think you have missed, however many mistakes you feel you have made or talents you think you don't have, or however far from home and family and God you feel you have traveled, I testify that you have not traveled beyond the reach of divine love. It is not possible for you to sink lower than the infinite light of Christ's Atonement shines" (Jeffrey R. Holland, "The Laborers in the Vineyard," *Ensign*, May 2012).

My friend Kris would tell you that He sees you even if you don't see Him. He can fill your hungry soul. He can help you to discover joy. He will meet you in your emptiness, your wandering, your dark places, there in your aching, and He will bring grace even if you don't know how it's done. You don't have to have a complete understanding for His grace to begin its work in you. The Lord will meet us in our ordinary places.

Just look for Him where you already are.

I don't know what your story looks like right now.
Maybe you feel overwhelmed, empty, discouraged.

Christ promises,

I will send grace to help in time of need.

Believe Christ.

"BUT THE GOD OF ALL GRACE . . . MAKE YOU PERFECT, STABLISH, STRENGTHEN, SETTLE YOU."

—1 PETER 5:10

chapter seven

My Grace Can Be Found in Wilderness Places

"AT THE SAME TIME, SAITH THE LORD,
WILL I BE THE GOD OF ALL THE FAMILIES OF ISRAEL,
AND THEY SHALL BE MY PEOPLE.
THUS SAITH THE LORD, THE PEOPLE . . .
FOUND GRACE IN THE WILDERNESS;
EVEN ISRAEL."

—JEREMIAH 31:1-2

My heart breaks for her every time I read her story—how she rose up early, and took bread and a bottle of water, and wandered with her young son into the wilderness. The water must have run out, the bread must not have lasted as long as she had hoped, because I read how she placed the child under a shrub in desperation, and then she walked away. To pray. To pour out her mother heart. "Let me not see the death of the child," she begged the Lord. And then, she wept (Genesis 21:16).

I read her story and I know why she weeps. I have almost lost a child. I have held an almost-lifeless body in my arms and pled to the Lord not to let me lose that boy. I have wept, wracking sobs that shook my body, and quiet tears into my pillow in the dark of night. I have felt the cold fear of not knowing how to save that little boy, and have said prayers that someone would know what I should do.

It is an angel whisper from heaven that calls to Hagar as she weeps, saying, "*Fear not; for God hath heard the voice of the lad where he is*. . . . And God opened her eyes, and she saw a well of water; and she went, and filled the bottle with water, and gave the lad drink" (Genesis 21:17–19; emphasis added).

Hagar found grace in the wilderness. A well in the midst of a desert place. As I read the story again, I discover that God's help didn't come just once. The next verse explains that God didn't take Hagar and her boy out of that wilderness place; instead He provided for them within the wilderness. He sent help into their wilderness through grace. "And God was with the lad; and he grew, *and dwelt in the wilderness*, and became an archer" (Genesis 21:20; emphasis added).

And sometimes God doesn't take away the wilderness.

. . .

Standing beside the pavilion I look out past the meadow, past the grass blowing slowly in the wind, past the trail that winds its way up, over, and around. I remember hearing the story, how this cove became a refuge from the winter storm, from the freezing temperatures, from the wind that whipped against the sagebrush, against a person's skin, against anything that lived. My eyes take in the rocks, the dirt, the rolling hills for as far as the eye can see.

The clouds overhead, the sagebrush along the trails, all of it looks the same.

It was October when the wind changed. It hinted of snow just before the sun went down. The wind whistled all through the night, chilling the moonlit plains. On October 19, 1856, the first flakes began to fall. Fourteen people died that night—forty-two more would follow in the next ten days. A gust of wind blew in winter and there were no shoes, no coats, no blankets. There was no refuge from the storm that stalked their souls. The temperatures dropped as the next storm rolled in, eleven degrees below zero. It would stall there, upon the people with no home. It would last for five days. Five hundred people on the plains, and nowhere to house them all. But the Lord had prepared a refuge. He had provided a cove.

The wind is still blowing, 160 years later, as I stand there and look out over the scene. The woman next to me is not dressed in a long skirt; she isn't there to remember those pioneers. She isn't even a member of The Church of Jesus Christ of Latter-day Saints. But she stands there just as enthralled by the cove as I am. She is here to study the land. She is a geologist.

"It's quite remarkable, isn't it?" She asks me.

I know why I think it is remarkable, but I wonder why she does. "What do you mean?" I ask her, all caught up in the question now.

"It's quite a phenomenon," she begins. "This is one of only three locations like this in the entire world." She explains to me how she is traveling to see each one of them. Then she lifts up her finger to show me the sandbar sitting right in the middle of the cove, how the terrain is set up in such a way that as the wind blew during the thousands and thousands of years since the earth was created, the sandbar was formed. "It's very rare," she tells me, "for a sandbar to form in the midst of a cove like this. The conditions have to be just right."

I look at the cove with different eyes now. What were the odds that five hundred people stranded on the plains would arrive at this precise location in the world on the eve of a five-day storm? That sandbar in the middle of the cove was situated in just the right location to provide shelter from the wind. It is what saved many lives that would have otherwise been lost. That unique sandbar is what made this particular cove a means of deliverance until the rescue came.

It is not the first time the Lord has provided a rescue by means of an unexplained phenomenon. When Moses and the children of Israel stood together with the army behind and the sea in front, the Lord provided a means of rescue by separating the waters and drying the ground. When Elisha and his servant were surrounded by an army intent on destroying them, the Lord sent chariots of fire down a mountainside. When a giant threatened to destroy an entire army, the Lord called upon an unlikely shepherd with five smooth stones. And when Hagar's bottle ran dry, He opened her eyes to see a well in the middle of her wilderness place.

When you think about God's grace, remember this: there is nothing that threatens the might of our God. He will use any means to rescue His people—a cove, chariots of fire, even a well in the middle of the wilderness. He is willing to redeem us at any cost.

It's true, God sent His own Son to rescue us. The Hebrew word for "redeem" is *padah*: "to preserve, deliver, or rescue, *by any means*." It is the last half of that definition that calls out to me.

By any means.

I am reminded of the scripture in Mosiah that testifies of Jesus Christ, saying, "*This is the means* whereby salvation cometh" (Mosiah 4:8; emphasis added). I consider the definition of grace in the Bible Dictionary, how we can receive strength to do good works that we otherwise would not be able to maintain if left to *our own means* (see Bible Dictionary, "Grace").

Even now, as I read through those two definitions, I am reminded of Jesus Christ. He *is* the means, and He will rescue us *by any means*. This doesn't mean that lives won't be lost, or hard things won't happen. But there will be moments in mortality when we will experience an unexpected refuge, a haven in the middle of our stormy times, when we will find grace in the wilderness. Martin's Cove is a testament of this.

I can't help but imagine the Creation, especially the separating of the mountains and the valleys. There is part of me that wonders if there might have been some discussion; *If I curve this mountain just like this, a sandbar will form. It will be ready for the winter day when Martin passes through with his company.* . . . I believe the Lord knew about the storm and the need for shelter long before Martin ever even built his handcart. Every time I hear the story, I am reminded of a Redeemer who would save His people *by any means*—even through a cove created in the middle of the Wyoming wilderness.

I can't help but wonder, *Where is your cove? Where is the well in your wilderness?* Where is the place God has designed for your refuge and for your rescue? Perhaps you could pull out a white piece of paper and look back over your life to see if you can find evidence of grace found in your wilderness places. Surely, it is there. Because, just as He did for Hagar and for Martin's Company, our God plans to ransom us, preserve us, and deliver us surely, and by any means, no matter what our wilderness looks like.

In the moments when we feel weak, discouraged, or destined to fail, we must remember the greatest Redeemer of all who has not left us to our own means. We can find His grace in the darkest storms, in our wilderness places, in our wandering. He has promised to rescue us, heal us, and deliver us by any means.

. . .

When Moses was in his wilderness place, the bush beside him burst into flame. "Moses, Moses," the Lord called from the midst of the bush. Moses answered, "Here am I" (Exodus 3:4). As the bush continued to burn, Moses bent down and pulled the leather sandals off his feet, and then he stood barefoot on holy ground. The Lord began to talk about the children of Israel. "I know their sorrows," He said, "and I am come down to deliver them" (vv. 7–8).

Moses found grace in his wilderness.

But the Lord didn't come into the wilderness just once.

Over and over within those first five books of the Bible I read how the children of Israel were led by this pillar of fire, led by the Lord. Grace found in the wilderness got them where they would

where is your cove?

never have gotten if left to their own means. In Moses's story, the Lord showed up in the wilderness as a pillar of fire.

Moses looked, and He was there.

When Joshua was in his wilderness, he lifted up his eyes and saw a man standing over him with his sword drawn in his hand. "Are you for us or against us?" Joshua questioned, and I can't help but wonder if fear filled up his heart. When the great soldier introduced himself to Joshua as the Lord, the captain of the host, Joshua bent down and pulled the leather sandals off his feet and then, like Moses had before him, he stood barefoot on holy ground (see Joshua 5:14–15).

The story reminds me that Joshua needed something different in his wilderness experience. For Joshua, who would conquer the promised land, the Lord didn't show up as a pillar of fire; instead He came as the captain of the host with sword in hand. He entered the story ready for exactly what Joshua would need.

And Joshua took off his shoes.

The lesson is not lost on me.

I pull out my white piece of paper and I begin to write what I know about the Grace Giver who shows up in each of our wilderness places, bringing exactly what we need. The Lord appeared as a pillar of fire for Moses and clothed in armor for Joshua. He came for Peter as a lifeguard, for the soldier in Gethsemane as a healer, and for His mother as a maker of wine. He met the woman at *her* well, the leper in *his* colony, and the daughter who was dead in *her very own* bedroom.

He entered their stories; He showed up ready for whatever their

grace

greatest need might be—to heal the hurt, to set free the captive, to guide through the wilderness, to win the battle, to prevent from loss, to preserve from disaster, to treat carefully, to strengthen from weariness, and to make safe from danger.

Grace found in the wilderness.

Just look, and it will be there.

I don't know what your story looks like right now.
Maybe you are searching for a well in your desert place,
a cove in your storm,
a pillar of fire in your bare feet.

Christ promises,

you can find grace in your wilderness
—grace to lead you, build you, keep you from stumbling
and cause you to stand.

Believe Christ.

"THE LORD REDEEMETH THE SOUL OF HIS SERVANTS:
AND NONE OF THEM THAT TRUST IN HIM
SHALL BE DESOLATE."

—PSALM 34:22

chapter eight

My Grace Will Much More Abound

"WHERE SIN ABOUNDED,
GRACE DID MUCH MORE ABOUND."

—ROMANS 5:20

When I walk into the room, I can't help but wonder about the circumstances that brought each person to this place. You aren't supposed to, but I do. I wonder what it is that chases them at night, the itch that can't be scratched, the gaping hole that nothing seems to fill. For four years I helped a friend shoulder the burden of addiction. The desperate late-night phone calls. The giving in. The sobbing in remorse. The wondering if you will ever find rest from this insatiable need that consumes every waking moment, and even the sleeping ones sometimes. I am exhausted from the weight, and the worry, and I am wearing thin. I look around the room and realize we all are worn thin. I long for the day when the Dark One will be bound.

It is the man who gathers us together that I am most intrigued by. We don't get to hear the stories of everyone in the room, but he shares his. How for his whole life he was chased, how he woke up every morning already running from the demon that would finally make him succumb. How he lived a life in chains, and bound up, and held captive. I feel the loss of freedom as he speaks. "And then," he says, with the first hint of hope lighting up his dark eyes, "I found this place."

I look around the room, at the people fully focused on the hope they see sparkling in his eyes. They are drawn to it, drawn to the possibility he speaks of. He describes how he comes to that room, to that circle of people, to this place of hope every single day. It's what allows him to sleep. To work. To have a family. He has found freedom because of the power in that room.

I am instantly intrigued.

I look around. There's nothing special about this room. It has brown carpet. The walls are white. It is used as a classroom in the daytime hours. There is a picture of Jesus hanging on one of the walls, and I don't know if it is always there or if it is hung up just for this. As I consider it all, I realize I might be wrong. There actually *is* something about the room. I felt it right when I walked in. Powerful. Abundant. Tangible. A feeling I have only felt with that kind of intensity one other time in my life, and it was when I was teaching in the prison.

What is it? I wondered. It wasn't hope, although it spoke of hope. It wasn't love, either, although it whispered love. It was an enabling strength I couldn't find words to describe—until I read the words of Paul. "But where sin abounded, grace did much more abound" (Romans 5:20).

I know what it is that draws that man there. Perhaps in the beginning it was the glitter of hope he saw in the eyes of his own facilitator. But that isn't what calls him back. It is the abundance of grace. The enabling power. The strength that tangibly fills the room and brings rest, and refuge, and reprieve.

Somehow, coming every day fills his reserves. This is a place of healing, a space for being made whole.

In this place, grace abounds.

. . .

There is only one lesson I remember from my physics class in college. Really, just one. Physics is the only class I received a D- in, the only class I ever almost failed. Now, after all of these years, Newton's third law is the only thing that I remember—how for every action, there is an equal and opposite reaction, which means the size of the force on the first object equals the size of the force on the second. I think to myself how God must know this law. How it is true of spiritual things, and not just physical things. How the Lord will compensate the force of evil with the force of grace. In abundance. Where sin abounds, grace abounds also. Much more than in regular situations. In force equal to the opposition it is up against.

Grace in abundance.

. . .

Across the Sea of Galilee you will find the country of the Gadarenes. It is a quiet place, with green, rolling hills. Removed. We drive through the countryside and I try to imagine the tombs and the man with no clothes who was tormented night and day.

When Jesus saw him, He looked past the devils and the torment and the wandering and simply asked for his name. *And all anyone ever saw were the devils.*

But not Jesus.

"Legion," the man answered Him, because he had been so long in this place, and maybe he had forgotten who he really was. He was Legion, a name that suggests 6,000 armed and strong warriors of evil. First, Jesus removed the distraction. There were pigs, and a cliff, and a lake, and then, there was silence. A man sitting at the feet of Jesus. Clothed, and in his right mind. I can't help but wonder where the clothes came from, and what the two of them talked about, and how the man felt to finally be at peace. What the man wanted most was to sit at Jesus's feet for the rest of his life. Just like the people in the room with the brown carpet and the white walls and the picture of Christ. There is safety that is felt in the abundance of grace. But Jesus told the man the healing would come by going back to his friends to tell the great things the Lord had done in his life and to talk about the Lord's compassion. And so, the man did. After Jesus left, the man went throughout the whole city and told "how great things Jesus had done unto him" (Luke 8:39).

I try to imagine that man's life before Jesus, before experiencing His grace. "Always, night and day, he was in the mountains, and in the tombs, crying, and cutting himself with stones" (Mark 5:5).

Then came grace.

Where he was.

And a life of chains, and being bound up, and held captive, and crying, and running from demons, was replaced with a testimony of how an abundance of grace can lead to great things. In those moments when you wonder if your past might destroy you, remember there is One who sees the good that might otherwise be concealed. He knows your name. He has great things in store for you. In that place where you feel bound, just remember, grace does much more abound.

I don't know what your story looks like right now.
Maybe you feel bound and fettered.
Maybe your past defines you.
Maybe you wonder if there is anyone who knows
who you really are deep down underneath it all.

Christ promises,
where sin abounds, grace will much more abound.
Believe Christ.

"IS ANY THING TOO HARD FOR THE LORD?"

—GENESIS 18:14

chapter nine

My Grace Will Keep You

"I AM MINDFUL OF YOU ALWAYS IN MY PRAYERS, CONTINUALLY PRAYING UNTO GOD THE FATHER IN THE NAME OF HIS HOLY CHILD, JESUS, THAT HE, THROUGH HIS INFINITE GOODNESS AND GRACE, WILL KEEP YOU THROUGH THE ENDURANCE OF FAITH ON HIS NAME TO THE END."

—MORONI 8:3

He was one of twenty-six students who had settled into his desk for the ninety minutes of third period. We were talking about how it would be possible to get back to the presence of God and how, exactly, the rescue would work. We had written several words on the white board—*Christ*, *Atonement*, *sacrifice*, *mercy*, *redeem*, *rescue*. One of the girls suggested we add *grace* to the list.

"But what does that even mean?" a student asked.

Another student chimed in, "Yes, what *is* grace?"

"It's a good question," I replied, looking at all twenty-six kids. "What do you think grace is?"

"It's an enabling power that comes through Christ," one replied.

"It's what makes up the difference," another added.

I watched the boy settled into the desk on the second row. I could see how he was thinking things through; I knew he would raise his hand even before he did. I could tell by the way his thoughts were coming together, the way the realization caught in his eyes. Once his hand popped up I looked over at him, knowing that what he said would be important. "Grace *is* what you cannot do." It was so simple and yet so powerful. It is one of the best definitions of grace I have ever heard.

. . .

When the news came about the great multitude that had gathered to come against them in battle, Jehoshaphat feared. I know that fear. The battle too great, the obstacle too hard to overcome. In that moment, Jehoshaphat gathered all of Judah, all of his people, to ask for help. They came together to seek the Lord.

They met at the Lord's house, because His name was in that house, and Jehoshaphat prayed, "O Lord God of our fathers, art not thou God in heaven? . . . and in thine hand is there not power and might, so that none is able to withstand thee? Art not thou our God?" *You promised us*, Jehoshaphat continued. "If, when evil cometh upon us, as the sword, judgment, or pestilence, or famine, we stand before this house, and in thy presence, (for thy name is in this house,) and cry unto thee in our affliction, then thou wilt hear and help" (2 Chronicles 20:6–9).

I imagine the people gathered there in front of the temple, *all of Judah*. I see the men prepared for battle standing before the Lord with their little ones, and their wives, and their children. I can hear the pleading in Jehoshaphat's prayer, "O our God . . . we have no might against this great company that cometh against us; *neither know we what to do*: but our eyes are upon thee" (2 Chronicles 20:12; emphasis added).

It is a prayer I have prayed a hundred times—Lord, I don't know what to do.

And how many times have you prayed that same prayer?

Then "came the Spirit of the Lord in the midst of the congregation . . . Thus saith the Lord unto you, Be not afraid nor dismayed by reason of this great multitude; for the battle is not yours, but God's. . . . Ye shall not need to fight in this battle . . . stand ye still . . . fear not, nor be dismayed . . . the Lord will be with you" (2 Chronicles 20:14–15, 17).

Then, from the Lord, came grace.

Grace to keep you. To protect you. To do what you cannot do. *This battle is not yours*, the Lord explained, *it is mine*. And I remember how the Lord promised that He, through grace, would keep us. In some translations, the word *keep* can be interchanged with *guard*, and maybe that is the Lord's reply. *Stand still, you don't need to fight this battle, I will be with you.* To guard you. To keep you.

Can you think of times when the Lord has stood guard over you? When His grace has kept you, protected you, held you safe?

Moments when He has fought a battle for you that you could never have fought alone? When, through grace, He has done what you could not do? Perhaps you might pull out a piece of paper and write those down.

. . .

I was walking down a crowded sidewalk in Egypt when I saw the baby bird, one who must have just fallen out of his nest. I saw the shoes of the passersby kicking it back and forth, scuffling up the dust, and no one looking down to see the little one floundering there. I fell right to my knees. Scooting between the people and the shoes and the dust, I reached until my hand captured the tiny thing, and I cradled it there in my cupped hand and wondered what to do. Behind me a rock wall, in front of me a busy road with horns blaring and cars swerving. There was nowhere for safety. No refuge. And then a young girl who lived there in the Egyptian city ran up to me, arms outstretched, her hands cupped together. "Here, here," she whispered. "My mama . . ." It was all the English she knew.

I placed the little bird carefully into her outstretched hands. "*Shukran*," I called after her. *Thank you.*

When I returned to the bus after our tour of an ancient Egyptian temple, the young girl was there waiting. She grabbed my hand. "My mama," she told me, nodding her head. I knew what she meant. The little bird was safe. She hugged me, and kissed my cheek, and I thought how we had just joined together in a rescue. As I sat down in my seat on the bus, the Spirit whispered, "Are not

moments of grace

five sparrows sold for two farthings, and not one of them is forgotten before God?" (Luke 12:6).

Do you ever need that reminder? *You have not been forgotten by God.* He has promised to keep you—keep you safe, keep you watched over, keep you protected through His grace.

God knows who we are, as tiny and insignificant as we might feel. We are precious to Him. Our value in His eyes is beyond our ability to comprehend. Where we see imperfections, He sees possibility. What we view as inadequate, He can turn into abundance. What we determine to be a failure, He knows is a proving ground for faith. *How is it done?* Through His grace. "Wherefore, if God so clothe the grass of the field . . . shall he not *much more* clothe you?" (Matthew 6:30; emphasis added). In those moments when we are faced with what we cannot do, we must remember that the Lord can enable us to do so *much more* than we could ever do on our own. Next time you don't have any more to give, when you feel inadequate or find yourself wondering if you will ever measure up, maybe you could remember this: Ours is the God of more, *much more.*

He wants to meet us where we are, in the middle of our story, to do for us what we cannot do on our own. *Not one will be forgotten before our God.* He sees our struggle, our weakness, and our pain. It doesn't matter if we are facing a great battle or are lost and broken on a crowded sidewalk, He will find us there and extend His grace to us. Scripture testifies that this is true.

. . .

Perhaps there are hard things you are battling right now. Things you carry, that only you know the depth of. We don't often talk about the hard things—the job we don't love, or how we are trying to manage a failing relationship, or the worry over how we will pay the bills. We don't talk about how we have set aside dreams and yearnings in order to meet the needs that are constantly pressing in, because that is the way life can be—constantly pressing in.

You know how it is.

Your little one who climbed into bed with you at 3:00 a.m. The teenager who causes you to water your pillow every night with fresh tears. The questions you ache to have answered. How there are so many people who need you, and life isn't simple, and many evenings find you worn out and used up.

And what about those ideas you carry in your heart? The gifts you've been given and hope to bring forth, but you don't know how or when because of all the juggling, and running late, and over-committing. Life isn't simple and sometimes you feel stuck, and the number of people you love and worry over keeps growing, and there isn't time enough for the prayers that should be prayed. And sometimes this looks like the life you chose, but much of the time it doesn't.

And maybe today you looked at your life and you didn't even know where to start.

Oh, dear friend, if that's where you are, then sit down for a minute, take a deep breath, and let me remind you of an important truth: *grace is what you cannot do.* His grace is what makes up for the lack, the imperfection, the falling short.

If He sees the sparrow on the sidewalk, He sees you.
Believe that He hears every prayer that you pray.
Believe that His Spirit is guiding your path.
Believe that you are already enough.
Let His grace keep you.

I don't know what your story looks like right now.
Maybe you are in an unexpected place.
Maybe you are afraid of what you are up against.
Maybe you need someone to fight your battle.

Christ promises,

my grace will keep you. Guard you. Protect you.

Believe Christ.

"AND GREAT GRACE WAS UPON THEM ALL."

—ACTS 4:33

chapter ten

My Grace Will Attend You

"TEACH YE DILIGENTLY
AND MY GRACE SHALL ATTEND YOU . . .
THAT YE MAY BE PREPARED IN ALL THINGS
WHEN I SHALL SEND YOU AGAIN
TO MAGNIFY THE CALLING
WHEREUNTO I HAVE CALLED YOU."

—D&C 88:78, 80

If I wake in the middle of the night, it's usually because I have been dreaming. My sleep is filled with vivid colors, intense conversations, and crazy things like trying to fit my toes into pink Barbie shoes so I don't have to walk through rain puddles in bare feet. My kids and my friends know about these dreams. They love to become my dream interpreters, because the colors and the conversations and the crazy things can't help but make you wonder what my subconscious is trying to uncover or work through or settle.

It is 2:00 a.m., and I am in the middle of a deep sleep, and somehow my daughter Meg and I have ended up in Jerusalem for the afternoon. I don't know how we got there, I am not sure why we only have one afternoon, but my subconscious isn't worried about details like those. In a split second I have to decide what I will show Meg in that one afternoon, and I immediately know where we should go. To the Old City. We will go shopping so she can see with her own eyes everything I love about the Jewish culture. The rituals. The remembering. The visuals attached to every religious undertaking. I will take her to the Temple Mount, and we will go to the Western Wall. She needs to go there; I feel it strongly. It has been a hard season, and she can write her prayer on a small piece of white paper like the Jewish women do, and fold it up into a tiny ball, and we will find a crack in the wall and push it in, and lean our forehead against the ancient stone, and we will pray.

I wake up from the dream in the darkest part of the night. I know the dream is important, but I am too tired to figure out why, so I leave myself a note on the paper I keep on the nightstand for moments such as these. Just three words: *Go to Jerusalem*. When I wake in the morning I will forget I had the dream until I see the note, and then I will remember and figure it all out.

It's several days before I see the note on the nightstand. The three words, *Go to Jerusalem*. I know they are important, but I can't remember why. And then, I remember the dream. Megan. The Old City. The Western Wall. The little white piece of paper. I think to myself how I can't take Meg to Jerusalem. I don't have enough money to get us there. We won't go see the little shops, or the Temple Mount, or the Western Wall. So why were those the three words I chose to remember the dream by? *Go to Jerusalem*. What did it mean?

I carry the paper around with me all day, thinking. When Meg comes home from work I tell her I had a dream about her. She smiles big in anticipation. Oh, my kids *love* when the dream is about them. She sits down. She knows about the colors and the conversations and the crazy things. She can't wait. I tell her the whole thing, about how we only had four hours. I describe the Old City with its small shops filled with prayer shawls, and frankincense, and menorahs. The men wearing *kippot*, how some have the *shel yad* wrapped around their arm and hand. I tell her how we spent the whole afternoon looking for a mezuzah for her door. I describe the Temple Mount, and the little white piece of paper, and the Western Wall with all of the women gathered there. I tell her how we prayed.

"When I woke up," I finish, "I wrote three words down to remember the dream. I think they are important, but I don't know why."

"What are the words?" she asks, ready as always to untangle the dream.

"*Go to Jerusalem.*" I recognize the importance as I say the words. "But we can't really go," I laugh as I tell her. "Neither you nor I have enough money."

"We don't need to go, Mom," she says. All is serious now. She starts speaking about the last season of her life. The painful things. "All of these hard days and the sleepless nights, all of the pain and the heartbreak, all of the not knowing what to do for the past few months has drawn me closer to Christ. I have already prayed the prayer I would have offered at the Western Wall. I have come to know Jesus better through this trial than I have my whole life. *This* has been my Jerusalem."

It is a profound statement.

I think back to my own Jerusalem moments. I know exactly what they are. The times when Jesus attended to me in my heartache. They are precious to me.

I can't help but wonder, *What is your Jerusalem? What has led you to know Jesus intimately?*

Perhaps you might take the time to write your own prayer and pleadings on a small piece of paper and pour out your desires to the Lord.

I remember a favorite quote: "We need not visit the Holy Land to feel him close to us. We need not walk by the shores of Galilee or among the Judean hills to walk where Jesus walked. In a very real sense, all can walk where Jesus walked when, with his words on our lips, his spirit in our hearts, and his teachings in our lives, we journey through mortality" (Thomas S. Monson, "The Paths Jesus Walked," *Ensign*, May 1974).

Yes, I have had my own "Go to Jerusalem" moments. Like Mary, I have had to choose the good part and sit at His feet. Like Peter, I have cried out when I was drowning. I have asked to see, just as the blind man did. I have doubted like Thomas. I have wept. I have reached. I have knelt. In my own ways, and in my own seasons, I have gone to Jerusalem. In my heart I have been there hundreds of times.

what is your Jerusalem?

Maybe you have, too. I don't know what is happening in your story right now. I wonder if there are heartbreaks, hard days, and sleepless nights? Perhaps you don't know what to do.

Go to Jerusalem.

Perhaps this trial has the potential to help you come to know Jesus in a way you haven't before.

. . .

He was no longer in Jerusalem.

The man was on the road to Jericho when trouble came, leaving him stripped, wounded, and half dead. I can't help but remember the thief, the priest, and the Levite. One caused harm, one saw him and walked on, and one looked on him and passed by. But there was one who came to where he was, and *this is the part of the story where grace begins.* The verses are clear—the Samaritan went to him. To bind up his wounds, to carry him to safety, to tend to him through the darkest hours of the night. The Samaritan offered grace where he was, this man who had left Jerusalem bound for Jericho.

Christ will do the same for us.

When we are wounded along the roadway of life, even if we are far away from the walls of Jerusalem, He comes to us "to bind up the brokenhearted, to proclaim liberty to the captives, and the opening of the prison to them that are bound . . . to comfort all that mourn . . . to give unto them beauty for ashes, the oil of joy for mourning, the garment of praise for the spirit of heaviness (Isaiah 61:1–3). He attends to us with His grace.

He is our Jerusalem.

It doesn't matter where we are or whether we are broken, bound, mourning, or heavy. His grace will attend to us, bringing beauty and joy in abundance.

I don't know what your story looks like right now.
Maybe you long for someone to tend to you and minister to you.
Go to Jerusalem.
Christ promises,
my grace will attend you.
Believe Christ.

"AND GOD IS ABLE TO MAKE ALL GRACE ABOUND TOWARD YOU."

—2 CORINTHIANS 9:8

chapter eleven

My Grace Will Accompany Peace and Good Hope

"NOW OUR LORD JESUS CHRIST HIMSELF,
AND GOD, EVEN OUR FATHER,
WHICH HATH LOVED US,
AND HATH GIVEN US EVERLASTING CONSOLATION
AND GOOD HOPE THROUGH GRACE,
COMFORT YOUR HEARTS, AND STABLISH YOU
IN EVERY GOOD WORD AND WORK."

—2 THESSALONIANS 2:16-17

It is winter. The dark comes too soon, and the cold surrounds, and I struggle to hold fast to joy. The storms that blew in with this season have been hard. They don't bring snow, or rain, or wind, but still they are bitter and they sting. I watch as my daughter's heart breaks; I see a son struggling against forces that would destroy him if it were possible. Every single day the storm rushes in—torrential, beating down, thundering, and I am worn and weary from the pounding. And why are people so cold?

The Psalmist describes a storm-filled wind with power to lift up the waves, how "they mount up to the [heavens]" and crash down again to the deep, and the people, "how their soul . . . [melts] because of trouble," and I wonder if He knows my life (Psalm 107:26). How we "reel to and fro," how we are "at [our] wits' end" (v. 27). They cried unto the Lord in their trouble, and we do too, and the Lord brings them out of their distress, to "their desired haven," and it is quiet there (v. 30). I can't help but wonder when we will find ours.

It is the Sabbath, and I sit on my pew, heart heavy and storm raging. In the prayer over the bread I am reminded that I have covenanted to take His name, and my soul is caught up in the wondering about this. *Which name?* the Spirit whispers to me. *Which name should you take?* I have never thought of it like this before. The boys in their white shirts with hair combed over, wearing Sunday shoes pulled on over basketball socks, those boys walk through the congregation passing the bread, and I turn to the Bible Dictionary, to the names of Christ. *Which one?*

Emmanuel. Mighty One. Carpenter. The Light. The Lord from Heaven. I know these names, but one stands out as different from the rest. *Shiloh.* I don't know this name. I search the meaning and I learn that in Hebrew the name means tranquil. It is exactly what I need, in the midst of this storm raging. I decide that for this week, this is the name I will take upon me. *Shiloh.* I read the verses in Genesis 49:10, how Shiloh will come, and I trust He will. Every single day, when the storm pushes in, when I am drowning, I whisper the name, *Shiloh*, and there is peace. The stilling of the storm. The promise of a quiet haven to come.

As the week continues I study the words *Shiloh*, *tranquil*, and *peace*. I find myself drawn over and over again to the words of Paul in the New Testament because I have discovered a pattern there: whenever Paul speaks of peace, he speaks of grace. Over thirty times I see the words together. They accompany each other, and I can't help but wonder why. What did Paul know about the synergy of peace and grace? I remember the two trees drawn on the white piece of paper earlier, the fruit that is labeled there, and I see peace and grace hanging from the branches. They are companion fruits of Christ, and perhaps the one is made complete in the other. And would that be true about charity, and hope, and rest, and joy? Does grace complete whatever it is companion to?

I spend the whole week studying the name I took during the sacrament, until I know it so well it becomes a part of me. The storm still surrounds, but Shiloh brings peace. And now I can't wait for the sacrament to come again. I wonder, *Which name will I take?* Which name will become part of me this next week?

And which name will you take?

Maybe you will place a piece of paper in your scriptures, just there, by your Bible Dictionary, next to the names of Christ. Perhaps it will become a journal of your weeks, and your names, and your storms, and His grace.

I drive through the snow of the most recent storm to visit a dear friend who is writing a song. It is our tradition when a song is born. I love to be introduced at the beginning. I sit on the chair next to the piano and watch her fingers move across the keys. The

take His name . . .

music pulls at my heart, the way it always does. The words speak to my soul.

I feel peace in the middle of my pain
I feel trust and hope even though my heart is aching
I can taste the bitter and sweet
Walking where the valley and the mountain meet
There is something so divine
When pain and grace collide
In the same place at the same time

—HILARY WEEKS, "IN THE SAME PLACE"

I know the peace and the trust within the pain. I know the aching. I know about the lowest valleys and the compassing about of mountain after mountain, and I wonder if I will ever summit those peaks. I know exactly what it feels like when pain and grace collide. I have been in that place more times than I can count. He has been there, too. Peace in the middle of my pain. *Shiloh.*

It is Sunday, and the boys walk through the pews, and the storms continue to rage, and I turn again to the Bible Dictionary. To the names of Christ. I read through the list slowly. *Which name?* There are so many to choose from, and as I read, an important truth settles itself into my heart. All those names? That is what grace looks like.

Every name I choose to take becomes a manifestation of His grace, and I am no longer afraid of the storm rolling in. I will take His name, and I will hope, and find peace in the promise of a quiet haven ahead.

I don't know what your story looks like right now.
Maybe you are in the middle of a painful place.
Perhaps your heart is aching.

Christ promises,

my grace will accompany peace, consolation, and good hope.

Believe Christ.

"GRACE AND PEACE BE MULTIPLIED UNTO YOU."

—2 PETER 1:2

chapter twelve

My Grace Will Transform You

"I AM THE LEAST OF THE APOSTLES,
THAT AM NOT MEET TO BE CALLED AN APOSTLE,
BECAUSE I PERSECUTED THE CHURCH OF GOD.
BUT BY THE GRACE OF GOD I AM WHAT I AM:
AND HIS GRACE WHICH WAS BESTOWED UPON
ME WAS NOT IN VAIN; BUT I LABOURED MORE
ABUNDANTLY THAN THEY ALL: YET NOT I, BUT
THE GRACE OF GOD WHICH WAS WITH ME"

—I CORINTHIANS 15:9-10

When the phone rings, it is a number I don't recognize. The man introduces himself as the president of the National Football League, and I don't tell him that I have never watched a professional game of football in my life. "We want to invite you and your husband to the first round of the NFL draft in Philadelphia," he says. "We have reserved a table in the green room for Garett. We'd like to bring you out. We're just so proud of your boy."

My mind immediately flashes back to August of 2011.

"What do you want me to do with Garett?" My husband has pulled over to the side of the road and called me from his cell phone. "He's standing on the curb with all of his stuff. I don't think he has anywhere to go." I tell Greg I will have to call him back, and then I walk into my room. I have two girls at home, a ninth-grader and a senior. Garett is eighteen. He is acquainted with drugs and alcohol. His friends are constantly in trouble with the law. Recently he spent some time in jail. It is a hard question. *What should we do with Garett?* It is a question I cannot answer on my own. I kneel down to pray.

The answer comes instantly. *Bring him home.*

So I call Greg, and they load up the back of the truck, and Garett moves in.

I focus back to the phone call with the man and the NFL. It's been five years now, and a life once filled with violence and vandalism and bad choices has slowly been molded by God. "Of course we will come," I tell him, and I hang up the phone with a smile and think to myself, *Who would have ever thought . . . ?*

A few weeks after that NFL phone call, a friend stops me in the parking lot. "I heard about Garett," he says with a smile. "That's really exciting for you, for your family."

"Yes, it is." I smile back, and then I tell him the truth of it, how it's all so surreal.

"Can I ask you a question?" he asks, eyes serious now. He sets his armful of stuff in his car and then turns around to talk to me again. "We've brought two boys into our home. My sister's kids. I see all the good things happening to Garett and I just want to know, *I'm just wondering*, in the beginning, in those first weeks, was it hard?"

Tears come instantly. I remember the heated late-night discussions, the letting go of all the bad friends, the setting of goals, the working through the demons and the damage of his past. I remember how every day in those beginning months I would ask the Lord, *What should we do with Garett?* and how the Spirit would answer back, *Just love him.* I blink back the tears that come from remembering just how hard it really was, and I tell him, "It's the hardest thing we've ever done."

"But are you better for it?" he hoped. I could see in his eyes how he sincerely wanted to know.

"I wouldn't be who I am," I told him. "That decision changed our life. It changed all of us."

. . .

We sit in the green room behind the black curtain at the NFL draft. There are eight of us, and none of us ever anticipated we would someday be there. Half of the room is full of a banquet table, piled high with food that no one can even eat. We are too nervous, all of us in this room, the boys, and the families, and the agents. One by one the teams draft their players, and between every new announcement the minutes tick by, and every boy sits at the table and wonders if someone will call his name.

There is a moment in the middle of the evening when Garett, his wife, Natalie, and I have a few minutes to talk. "What if they don't call my name, Mom? This is my dream, and what if no one calls my name?"

I remember looking at this boy I had come to love with my whole heart, this boy who had always dreamed he would play in the NFL, the boy who'd had to talk me into believing in that dream. "Garett, you *are* living your dream," I tell him, still incredulous that we are sitting in the green room of the NFL draft. "You are going to play in the NFL. You did it. The fact that we are sitting at this table in this room is a testimony of that. Now, we have to be patient and let God do His work. He knows the right team for you. He knows where your family is meant to live. When the timing is right, the right team will call your name. We have to believe that."

It is about five minutes later when a television cameraman comes and stands next to our table, lens fixed on Garett. Then another one comes, and another. I look at Garett's agent with questioning in my eyes; I don't want to get my hopes up if it isn't the right time. The agent raises his shoulders—*I don't know.* It is the twentieth pick of the first round of the 2017 NFL Draft. The Broncos are on the clock. And now there are eight cameras around the table, and Garett's phone starts to ring. "It's a Denver number," his wife says, her voice shaking with excitement. That's when Garett starts to cry. "Answer it," she whispers, and so he does. It's John Elway on the other side of the phone, inviting Garett to become a Bronco. There are a lot of tears, and a lot of hugging, and Garett is called down to the main stage, and they want him to bring his baby with him. And then we are standing in front of the TV in the green room, and Garett and baby Kingston are on the stage on the other side of the black curtain, and we watch Garett holding a Denver Broncos jersey in one hand and his baby in the other.

The man with a microphone tells Garett how much he admires his story, how incredible it is that someone from his background—a learning disability, time in jail, the struggles of his youth—would make it to the NFL. He wonders how it happened. I'll never forget Garett's reply: "By the grace of God I am here."

And it was completely true.

People think it was Greg who met Garett on the curb that day in August 2011, but really, it was the Lord. He met Garett where he was, as he was, but He didn't intend to leave him there. He extended grace, and surrounded Garett with exactly what he needed to become exactly who God knew He could be.

It's who God is.

It's what the grace of God does.

Garett's isn't the only story the Lord entered into. Every time I remember Garett standing on the stage of the NFL draft, I think of the words of Paul: "I am the least of the apostles, that am not meet to be called an apostle, because I persecuted the church of God. *But by the grace of God I am what I am:* and his grace which was bestowed upon me was not in vain; but I labored more abundantly than they all: yet not I, but the grace of God which was with me" (1 Corinthians 15:9–10; emphasis added).

And so, we come full circle. Somehow Christ's grace turned the life of a troubled teen around, the same way it did for a man breathing out threatenings on the road to Damascus.

This is grace.

A gift that comes from God and through the Atonement of Christ. A gift extended by coaches, and neighbors, and friends. An enabling power that strengthened a boy to do what he could not have done on his own. There is no other way to describe the miracles that led to this boy standing on the stage at the NFL draft; it's simply by grace.

I don't know exactly how it works, but I know it does.

. . .

It is important to remember that there are places we would never be able to reach if left to our own devices. No matter how appealing the destination, how worthy the dream, there are places we are not capable of reaching if left to our own means. This is the power of Christ's grace; this then is the reason for grace.

I am reminded once again about the tightrope walker with the wheelbarrow, Charles Blondin, and of another journey he took across Niagara Falls. It is my favorite of all his journeys. This time, Blondin is about to attempt something he hasn't before—he stands at the very edge of the Canadian border with his manager, Harry Colcord, clinging to his back.

Again, the rope has been strung 1,100 feet across. The guylines have been attached every twenty feet in an effort to steady the rope from the oncoming wind. However, in the very middle, there is fifty feet of freestanding rope, without guylines, because it was impossible to anchor them there. For this part of the journey, there will be no safety from the wind.

Blondin and Colcord begin the journey in silence. Then, just as they approach the last guyline before the fifty feet of free-hanging rope, Blondin turns to his friend. "Look up, Harry. For the next fifty feet you are no longer Colcord, you are Blondin. If I sway, sway with me. Do not attempt to do any balancing on your own. If you do, we will both fall to our death." Then Blondin took the next step, and the next, until finally he and Harry made it all the way across, with only a few guylines snapping along the way.

I think about the significance of the journey—how Blondin took Harry to a place he would never have been able to get to on his own, how he delivered him safely there, and I can't help but ask myself this one question: *Who did the work?* Only one was responsible for the delivering, the finishing, the carrying safely across, because only one was capable of accomplishing that task. Harry's feet never touched the rope; it was Blondin who did that work. Harry was responsible for believing in Blondin, for clinging to him with all of his might, mind, and strength, for trusting him enough to move with him as he moved, for centering himself firmly on the deliverer.

Perhaps we will all experience times like these. Moments when we cling to the Lord with all of our heart, might, mind, and strength and center ourselves on Him through our belief. It is when we learn to find balance in Him and trust His grace that the transformation begins.

This, my friend, is the knowledge that I want you to hold on to. The Lord will meet you where you are, as you are, but He doesn't intend to leave you there. Through His grace, the Lord will take you to places you could never go on your own.

I don't know what your story looks like right now.
Where would you like to be? Who would you like to become?

Christ promises,

my grace will strengthen you and enable you to
become who God knows you can become.
My grace has the power to transform you.

Believe Christ.

"LOVE GOD WITH ALL OF YOUR MIGHT,
MIND AND STRENGTH,
THEN IS HIS GRACE SUFFICIENT FOR YOU."

—MORONI 10:32

Come Broken

Have you ever had times when you keep hearing about the same thing over and over again? Maybe it's a scripture that you keep running across, or a quote that keeps jumping out at you, or a story people seem to keep retelling everywhere you go. My friend calls this phenomenon a soul echo; she believes the repetition comes because there is a lesson that your soul needs to learn, and lately my soul has been learning about grace.

It probably won't surprise you that I have been experiencing a soul echo. I keep running across the lesson of *Kintsugi*, "golden joinery." Perhaps you have seen it also. It's the Japanese art of repairing a broken piece of pottery with golden lacquer. Many believe that the piece is more beautiful because it was broken, and it is true—the bright ceramic pieces with the gold etching throughout really are breathtaking.

And why are we so afraid of being broken?

It's probably because of this soul echo that when I opened the package from off the front porch and saw the vase lying in pieces at the bottom, my first thought was to repair it. I knew right when I picked up the box that something wasn't right. I could hear the pieces rattling inside. Vases shouldn't rattle. So, I wasn't surprised to find the vase lying in twenty-nine pieces at the bottom. There was a gasp of disappointment, but immediately desire filled my heart. I wanted to try this *Kintsugi*. I wanted to see what I would learn. And so, I began.

There were things I didn't realize, would never have realized, had I not entered into the learning. A joinery cannot happen in one afternoon. It takes place over days; it could take weeks. The vase must be repaired one piece at a time. First there is the process of searching, trying piece after piece until you find the right shape to fit into the empty place. Then, there is the gluing—holding it fast and letting it dry until there is strength. The process can't be rushed; this strengthening takes time. If you put too many pieces into place at once, the vase falls into brokenness again. It must happen step by step, piece by piece, grace for grace.

Every morning for weeks I would wake up and walk into the room where the vase was waiting. The sunlight spilled onto the table where I worked, illuminating the process. Before I started working, I would check the joinery from the day before, testing the strength of it. And then, I would begin the search for the next right piece. It was weeks before the vase was finished. The process took time. Then, one day, the last piece was finally fitted into the top, and the vase was whole again.

Some will look at the vase and see the damage there. But I don't. I look at each piece and see the story it has to tell—about the

come broken

getting found, the holding fast, and the strengthening. The vase has become a reminder to me of the Lord's grace, of how it works, because there are times in my own life when I have been in twenty-nine pieces. What I have longed for most in those moments is for my life to be put back together in one afternoon. It has never happened that way. The Savior allows us to come broken. He sits with us and mends our hearts. He offers healing. He extends an enabling power that gives us strength beyond our own. He fills the empty places. He makes what was broken strong again. This is the process of grace, and it has taught me an important truth. Grace is not an event; it's a story.

You have a story, and I have a story, and each of our stories is different, but one thing is constant in all of them. Jesus. He was God's plan from the very beginning. Long before we were born, our loving Father planned for our leaving, but He also planned for bringing us Home. He didn't send us to earth alone. He sent His Son to be with us, to walk with us, to enter our stories, and to put our twenty-nine pieces back together, one broken piece at a time.

We receive His grace when we invite Him to work within those broken places—when we allow for the finding, the holding fast, and the strengthening to happen from grace to grace. He is the Grace Giver, and His gift is to transform lives, and change hearts, and heal. *He wants to heal us.*

It doesn't matter how empty your reserves.

It doesn't matter how deep the dark place.

It doesn't matter how far you have wandered.

It doesn't matter how discouraging the ache.

He will meet you in that place. He will enter your story. He will send grace where you are.

I don't know what your story looks like right now, but He does. Perhaps you are the criminal on the cross, the woman in the temple courtyard, the father with the son who can't be healed, the man intent on destroying all that is good. You might be clinging to the back of a tightrope walker or seeking cover in a cove in the middle of Wyoming. He sees you there, just as He sees the blind woman teaching the class, the two girls on a couch, the boy in the green room of the NFL draft, and the lost three-year-old in the wilderness waiting next to a rock. It doesn't matter where you are in your story; He will meet you there, and through grace He will take you to places you could never go on your own. He will shield you, succor you, heal you, and make you whole. He will defend you, help you, rescue you, and deliver you surely, and by any means. It is His mission to hand you safely over to His Father. Yes, the Lord will meet you where you are, as you are, but He doesn't intend to leave you there. He's going to walk you home.

Sometimes I imagine what that moment might be like, the coming home. I picture a glorious reunion. There is a lot of hugging, and crying, and gratitude, and peace that comes from knowing the journey is over. I am certain there will be looking back, and remembering. *My mind always pauses on the remembering.* Already I can think of the experiences of this life journey that will stand out to me, the times when the Savior has come to deliver me, redeem me, and rescue me. Those moments are held fast in my heart, and I imagine those are the memories He and I will talk about. My twenty-nine-piece moments. The times when He put me back together again, from grace to grace. I will share the parts of my story where grace and pain collided and I was made whole again, and you will too, and it will amaze us how Jesus was able to do that for each of us. It will be a long conversation, a catching up, and perhaps at the end we will each look back over our journey and say, just as Paul did, "By the grace of God I am what I am" (1 Corinthians 15:10).

By His grace.

The grace that elevates souls and heals wounds.

The grace that meets us where we are.

Come broken, my friend, but then hold on to His grace. Cling to it. Receive it into your heart and let it wash over you and make you whole. It is His gift.

Live in grace.

The Lord will take you to places you could never go on your own.

"THE GRACE OF OUR LORD JESUS CHRIST BE WITH YOU ALL."

—REVELATION 22:21

Christ promises,

My grace has the power to mend and heal you.
My grace can overcome brokenness and weakness.
My grace has the power to deliver and preserve you—
to rescue, to defend, to succor, to shield,
and to hand you safely over to God.
I will send grace to help in time of need, He says.
Grace in your wilderness.
Grace to lead you, build you, keep you
from stumbling, and cause you to stand.
Where sin abounds, my grace will much more abound.
My grace will keep you. Guard you. Protect you.
My grace will attend you.
My grace will accompany peace, consolation, and good hope.
My grace will strengthen you and enable you to
become who God knows you can become.
My grace has the power to transform you.

Believe Christ.

"THOU THEREFORE . . . BE STRONG IN THE
GRACE THAT IS IN CHRIST JESUS."

2 TIMOTHY 2:1

Acknowledgments

Life has taught me that grace is a story. It's my story, and it's your story. For that reason, the pages of this book are filled to overflowing with stories. Some of them you will be familiar with—the woman caught in adultery, the man at the Gadarenes, the father who came searching for healing for his son. But there are many others who you will discover for the first time. Heartfelt thanks to those who either shared their stories or shared their wisdom as the pages of this book were filled up, worked through, and crafted, including Carl W. Bond, Tasha Murphy, Chrislyn Woolsten, Hilary Weeks, Robin Merrill, Kris Belcher, David Butler, Janaye Freeman, Samantha Murphy, Megan Lund, Misty, Maki, and Andrew, Sean, and Doug Parry. Words cannot express my gratitude to Allison Kimball for the beautiful care she took with the artwork in this book. Besides being a talented illustrator, you are a dear friend. Thank you for your gift. Also, an abundance of gratitude for Robert Millet, a dear friend who spent hours discussing the topic of grace with me. To the team at Deseret Book, including Laurel Christensen Day, Tracy Keck, Lisa Roper, and Heather Ward, thank you for your talents and your dedication to building the Kingdom. I love working shoulder to shoulder with you.

About the Author

Photo by Hunter Fowler

EMILY BELLE FREEMAN is a best-selling author and popular inspirational speaker. She has a deep love of the scriptures, which comes from a desire to find their application in everyday life. She is the author of numerous books, including *Creating a Christ-Centered Home; Closer to Christ;* and *Even This: Getting to the Place Where You Can Trust God with Anything.* She is a favorite speaker at Time Out for Women and a cohost with David Butler of *Don't Miss This,* a "Come, Follow Me" study channel on YouTube. Her greatest joy comes from spending time with her family. Read more at emilybellefreeman.com and follow Emily on Instagram and Facebook @emilybellefreeman.